Ranjith P.Nathan
3590 Kaneff Cr, Suite 1606
Mississauga
Ont L5A-3X3
CANADA

Concise Guide to

MS-DOS®
BATCH
FILES

Microsoft
PRESS

KRIS JAMSA

PUBLISHED BY
Microsoft Press
A Division of Microsoft Corporation
One Microsoft Way
Redmond, Washington 98052-6399

Library of Congress Cataloging-in-Publication Data.
Jamsa, Kris A.
    Concise guide to MS-DOS batch files / Kris Jamsa.--Rev. for
version 6.2.
        p.   cm.
    Includes index.
    ISBN 1-55615-638-3
    1. Operating systems (Computers)   2. MS-DOS (Computer file)
3. Electronic data processing--Batch processing.   I. Title.
QA76.76.O63J32   1993
005.4'469--dc20   93-38176
                                                        CIP

Printed and bound in the United States of America.

1 2 3 4 5 6 7 8 9   AG-M   9 8 7 6 5 4

Distributed to the book trade in Canada by Macmillan of Canada, a division of
Canada Publishing Corporation.

Distributed to the book trade outside the United States and Canada by Penguin
Books Ltd.

Penguin Books Ltd., Harmondsworth, Middlesex, England
Penguin Books Australia Ltd., Ringwood, Victoria, Australia
Penguin Books N.Z. Ltd., 182–190 Wairau Road, Auckland 10, New Zealand

British Cataloging-in-Publication Data available.

Acquisitions Editor: Mike Halvorson
Project Editors: Tara Powers-Hausmann, Pam Horino
Technical Editors: Stuart Stuple, Mary DeJong
Manuscript Editor: Online Press
Principal Typographer: Bill Teel

Contents

Introduction

For many years, experienced MS-DOS users have used MS-DOS batch files to save them time and keystrokes. Unfortunately, new users who can often benefit the most from batch files are never really taught how to use them. As such, this book introduces MS-DOS batch files, beginning first with the basics. As your understanding and confidence grows, this book will present more advanced topics that let you unleash your computer's full potential. Experienced batch-file users will learn how to add color and line-drawing characters to the screen display generated by their batch files. This book will also present the new batch-file commands introduced with MS-DOS 6. In addition, you will learn how to control your system configuration using menu options that select CONFIG.SYS entries and how to use batch files with Microsoft Windows!

Put simply, an MS-DOS batch file is a file that contains MS-DOS commands. When you type the name of a batch file at the command prompt, MS-DOS executes the commands that the batch file contains. Many users employ simple batch files on a daily basis, abbreviating a series of commonly used commands. As you will learn, however, most users fail to take full advantage of the potential that batch files offer.

Although the MS-DOS commands are quite powerful, there are times when the commands still don't provide you with all the capabilities you need. As such, this book provides you with all that you need to know about creating your own batch files. The presentation starts at the very beginning, with instructions for creating your batch files using the MS-DOS editing tools, and then guides you through each of the batch-file commands. Each command is introduced with a detailed explanation and then described in a practical example. You'll also learn a number of advanced batch-file techniques such as testing exit conditions with the IF ERRORLEVEL statement, obtaining user responses with the MS-DOS version 6 CHOICE command, and using named parameters. You'll then learn how to put the commands together to perform a variety of useful tasks as you begin to build your own batch-file library. Best of all, these programs take only minutes to create. You don't need any special programming languages—all you need is MS-DOS!

If you are using MS-DOS version 5 (or later), this guide teaches you how to create macro definitions using the DOSKEY command. A macro is similiar to an MS-DOS batch file in that it contains the names of one or more commands you can execute by simply typing the macro name. Unlike MS-DOS batch files, macros reside in your computer's fast electronic RAM (random-access memory) instead of on disks. If you are using MS-DOS 5 (or later), knowledge of the DOSKEY command will make you immediately more productive.

One of the most important batch files on your system is AUTO-EXEC.BAT. This file, which is used to configure your system, is discussed in detail. Beginning with version 6, MS-DOS provides a set of entries you can place within your CONFIG.SYS file that allow you to better control how MS-DOS loads itself into memory. This book shows you how to use each of these entries. By following the examples presented, you can quickly create custom menus that MS-DOS displays each time your system starts and that let you select the configuration you desire. As you will find, like MS-DOS batch files, the CON-FIG.SYS customization entries are very easy to use once you know a few secrets.

You don't have to be an expert to use this guide. Any MS-DOS user can easily follow the examples. Learning how to create and use batch files and DOSKEY macros might just be the most productive time you spend at your computer. Regardless of the tasks you normally perform with your computer, batch files and macros can save you time! This book is filled with batch-file secrets that are unavailable elsewhere. So let's get started.

CHAPTER I

Getting Started with Batch Files

UNDERSTANDING BATCH-FILE PROCESSING

The number of MS-DOS commands now exceeds 80. Most of us, however, use only a small subset of these commands, such as COPY, REN, DEL, TYPE, DISKCOPY, and FORMAT—and possibly the subdirectory commands. We probably can't recall the format for many of the other commands, let alone their command-line switches.

To accomplish tasks such as moving to a specific directory and running a word processor, novice users often have to perform a series of commands. As the amount of typing you must perform increases, so too does the possibility of error. An error can be the omission of a critical command, or it can be a typographical error.

To simplify the use of MS-DOS and decrease the likelihood of error, MS-DOS supports batch files. A batch file is a file you create that contains one or more MS-DOS commands. To execute all the commands in a batch file, you simply type the name of the batch file at a command prompt and press the Enter key, exactly as if the batch file were a single MS-DOS command. MS-DOS then executes all the batch-file commands, starting with the first command and working toward the last.

To see how batch files work, let's examine a batch file named TIME-DATE.BAT that contains three basic MS-DOS commands:

```
CLS
TIME
DATE
```

You will create a batch file similiar to this one later; for now, we'll simply discuss how it works.

1

CLS clears the screen display; TIME displays the current time and prompts you to enter a new time; and DATE displays the current date and prompts you to enter a new date.

Notice the BAT filename extension. Filename extensions can describe the type of information a file contains. In the case of TIMEDATE.BAT, the BAT extension tells you, as well as MS-DOS, that the file is a batch file. To run the batch file, you type the name of the batch file at the command prompt and then press the Enter key, as follows:

```
C:\> TIMEDATE
```

When MS-DOS encounters the name of the batch file, it opens the batch file and executes the first command in the file—in this case, CLS. After the CLS command completes execution, MS-DOS executes the next command in the batch file—TIME. At this point, MS-DOS displays the following:

```
C:\> TIME
Current time is 3:26:46.03p
Enter new time:
```

You now type the correct time and press the Enter key, or you press Enter to leave the time unchanged. After TIME completes execution, MS-DOS executes the DATE command and displays the following:

```
C:\> DATE
Current date is Thu 04-07-1994
Enter new date (mm-dd-yy):
```

You now type the correct date and press Enter, or you press Enter to leave the date unchanged. When the DATE command completes execution, MS-DOS searches for the next command in the batch file. Because no other commands exist, the batch file completes execution, and MS-DOS displays its prompt.

NOTE: *MS-DOS versions earlier than 4.0 do not support the 12-hour clock. Such versions would not display a p for P.M., as shown above. Instead, those versions would display 15:26:46.03. This book is based on MS-DOS versions 6 and later unless otherwise noted.*

Let's examine another batch file, DISKINFO.BAT, which contains three MS-DOS commands:

```
VOL
CHKDSK
DIR
```

To execute the commands in this file, which display information about the current drive, you type the name of the batch file and press Enter:

```
C:\> DISKINFO
```

NOTE: *If MS-DOS displays the message* Bad command or file name *when you execute this batch file, MS-DOS could not locate the CHKDSK.EXE external command. External commands must reside in the current directory or be accessible via the path defined by the MS-DOS PATH command in your AUTOEXEC.BAT file.*

ADVANTAGES OF BATCH FILES

MS-DOS batch files save you time, reduce keystrokes and errors, and simplify the execution of difficult commands. As you become more comfortable with batch files, they will become important tools that make your time at the computer more productive. To see how, let's look at several batch-file examples.

Saving Time

Assume that each morning you must run four inventory-control programs. The first program, CALCINV.EXE, calculates your current product inventory. The second, SORTINV.EXE, sorts the inventory by quantity on hand. The third, PRINTINV.EXE, prints listings of inventory quantities on hand. The fourth, ORDERINV.EXE, generates purchase orders for items that need to be stocked.

To run these four programs, you must type the name of the first program, press the Enter key, and wait for the program to complete execution before repeating these steps for the remaining programs. You might spend a considerable amount of time sitting at the keyboard and waiting for each program to finish its job.

These commands are excellent candidates for a batch file. In this case, you might name the batch file GETINV.BAT. This file contains the four commands:

```
CALCINV
SORTINV
PRINTINV
ORDERINV
```

When you type the name of the batch file and press Enter, MS-DOS sequentially executes the four commands for you, displaying the output of each command:

```
C:\> GETINV

C:\> CALCINV
...Calculating current product inventory

C:\> SORTINV
...Sorting inventory by quantity

C:\> PRINTINV
...Printing inventory

C:\> ORDERINV
...Generating purchase orders
```

While MS-DOS executes the commands, you are free to perform other tasks away from your computer. In this way, using a batch file can save considerable time each day.

Saving Keystrokes and Reducing Errors

Because batch files allow you to execute multiple commands by entering one command name, they reduce the number of keystrokes you must enter, which directly reduces the possibility of error. In the previous example, executing the GETINV.BAT batch file not only reduced the number of keystrokes but also eliminated the possibility of executing commands in the wrong order, typing a command incorrectly, or omitting a command.

Simplifying Command Execution

We were all new to MS-DOS at one time. Most of us can remember the intimidation we felt when we issued our first MS-DOS commands. Batch files help to minimize this intimidation by reducing the number of difficult commands that someone new to MS-DOS must remember and successfully execute. For example, most of us keep our word-processing document files in a unique subdirectory. To run the word processor and conveniently access those files, you must first select the correct subdirectory by using the CHDIR (Change Directory) command and then select the word processor. In the case of Microsoft Word, for example, the sequence of commands becomes something like the following:

```
C:\> CHDIR \DOCS
```

```
C:\> WORD
```

Whether you are a new user or an experienced user who is helping a beginner, you might consider creating a batch file named DOCS.BAT that contains both commands. The fewer commands new users must memorize, the more comfortable they will feel with the computer. As a result, they will learn faster.

NAMING BATCH FILES

You should always try to give meaningful filenames to every file you create. Batch files are no exception. MS-DOS batch files must have the BAT extension. As a result, you have only the eight-character filename to distinguish one batch file from another. The name of the batch file should clearly explain the processing that the batch file performs. For example, earlier we examined the TIMEDATE.BAT batch file, which set your system's time and date; and in our inventory example, the batch file was GETINV.BAT. Both of these batch-file names explain the processing the files perform. Although naming a batch file X.BAT or Z.BAT is easy, neither name describes what the batch file does. A few days after you create such a batch file, you probably won't recall its function.

Avoid giving a batch file the same name as an internal MS-DOS command or an external command (identified by the EXE or COM extension). Although batch files are also considered commands by MS-DOS, if MS-DOS encounters an internal or external command first, it executes that command instead of the batch file. MS-DOS never executes a batch file with the same name as an MS-DOS internal command and only executes a batch file with the same name as an external command in very particular circumstances.

Each time you type a command at the command prompt, MS-DOS first checks to see if your command is an internal command (such as CLS, DATE, or TIME), which MS-DOS keeps in memory at all times. If your command is an internal command, MS-DOS executes it (instead of any external command, including your batch file). For example, if your batch file is named TIME.BAT, MS-DOS locates the TIME command and executes only this internal command.

If MS-DOS finds that the command is not an internal command, it then tests to see if the command is an external command in the current directory. An external MS-DOS command (such as DISKCOPY or FORMAT) is an MS-DOS command that resides on disk. Other external commands include those used to start programs (such as WORD.EXE or WIN.COM). If MS-DOS finds an external command with the name you typed, it executes that command.

Finally, if your command is not an internal command in memory or an external command on disk, MS-DOS tests to see if your command corresponds to an MS-DOS batch file in the current directory. MS-DOS executes batch files only if it encounters no matching internal or external command in the current drive and directory.

Suppose no command matching the filename is located in the current directory. MS-DOS then begins to search the directories specified on your search path. It checks each directory (in the order specified), first for an external command and then for a batch file. A batch file is executed only if MS-DOS finds the batch file with the specified filename before encountering an external command with the same name. (In Chapter 2, we discuss how to set your search path in your AUTOEXEC.BAT file.)

To summarize, if you assign the batch file the name of an internal MS-DOS command, the batch file never executes. If you assign the batch file the name of an external command, MS-DOS might execute the batch file or the external command depending on which file it encounters first.

CREATING BATCH FILES

The method you choose to create a batch file will vary depending on its length. For short batch files, the simplest and fastest method is to copy the batch file from the keyboard. To do this, you perform a copy operation using CON (the device name for the keyboard) as the source of your batch file's input. As a demonstration, we will create the TIMEDATE.BAT batch file, which sets the system time and date. To begin the batch-file copy operation, type the following command at the command prompt:

```
C:\> COPY CON TIMEDATE.BAT
```

MS-DOS then performs a copy operation using the COPY command. In this case, the source of the data to copy is the keyboard. The target of the copy operation is the TIMEDATE.BAT batch file. When you press the Enter key to begin the copy operation, MS-DOS places the cursor at the start of the line following the command. At this point, MS-DOS is waiting for the first line of input. Type the command *TIME*, which is the first command in this batch file, and press Enter:

```
C:\> COPY CON TIMEDATE.BAT
TIME
```

Next type the command *DATE*, and press Enter:

```
C:\> COPY CON TIMEDATE.BAT
TIME
DATE
```

The DATE command is the last command in the batch file. You must tell MS-DOS that you have no more input for the file. To do so, press the F6 (end-of-file) function key, and then press Enter. MS-DOS displays the characters ^Z at the bottom of your batch file. (Caution: Do not press Shift-8 to create the caret. Alternatively, you can hold down the Ctrl key and press Z to create ^Z.)

The ^Z characters, pronounced *Control Z*, indicate the end of the file to MS-DOS. When you press Enter following ^Z, you tell MS-DOS that you have completed the copy operation. As a result, MS-DOS creates the batch file and displays the following:

```
C:\> COPY CON TIMEDATE.BAT
TIME
DATE
^Z
        1 File(s) copied

C:\>
```

To execute this batch file, type *TIMEDATE*:

```
C:\> TIMEDATE
```

When you press Enter, MS-DOS executes first the TIME command and then the DATE command.

Now use the COPY CON technique to create a batch file named DISKINFO.BAT that contains the commands VOL, CHKDSK, and

DIR. As before, type the COPY command line, using the CON device name as your input source, and press Enter:

```
C:\> COPY CON DISKINFO.BAT
```

Next type each batch-file command, pressing Enter after each command name:

```
C:\> COPY CON DISKINFO.BAT
VOL
CHKDSK
DIR
```

To tell MS-DOS you're finished entering commands, press the F6 key, and then press Enter. MS-DOS creates the batch file and tells you that one file has been copied:

```
C:\> COPY CON DISKINFO.BAT
VOL
CHKDSK
DIR
^Z
        1 File(s) copied

C:\>
```

To summarize, you can create small batch files from the keyboard by following these steps:

1. Issue a COPY command using CON as the source and using a meaningful name for the batch file as the target. Then press Enter. For example:

   ```
   C:\> COPY CON DATEPRNT.BAT
   ```

2. Type one batch-file command at a time, and press Enter after each command.

3. After typing the last batch-file command, press the F6 key, and then press Enter. (F6 signals the end of the file to MS-DOS.)

Creating Larger Batch Files

As your batch files get larger, you will want to use a word processor, the full-screen MS-DOS Editor (provided with MS-DOS versions 5 and later), or the Edlin line editor (provided with versions of MS-DOS earlier than 5). If you use a word processor, be sure to save the file in a text-only (ASCII) format. As you probably know, word processors allow you to format text in various ways, such as changing the font or size of specific characters or changing the alignment of specific paragraphs. To perform these tasks, word processors embed characters within your file. Although these embedded characters are meaningful to the word processor, MS-DOS does not understand them. If these characters appear in your batch files, they cause errors. If you save your word-processing files in ASCII format, the word processor does not embed these characters.

Creating a Batch File with Edit

MS-DOS versions 5 and later include the MS-DOS Editor, also called Edit. Edit is a full-screen editor (meaning it lets you use the entire screen) that allows you to create and change files. To understand how Edit works, let's use it to create a batch file named SHORTDIR.BAT that contains the CLS and DIR /W commands.

To begin, run Edit from the command prompt, and specify the name of the file you want to work with. If the file does not yet exist, it will be created. If you do not specify a filename, an untitled document is created and you must specify a name when you save the file. For this example, the following is your command line:

```
C:\> EDIT SHORTDIR.BAT
```

When you press Enter, Edit displays the screen shown in Figure 1-1.

The blinking underscore in the upper left corner is the cursor, which indicates where characters will appear as you type them. Centered above the area you type in is the name of the file, SHORTDIR.BAT. (If you did not specify a filename on the command line, you see the word

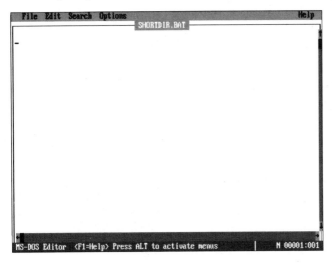

FIGURE 1-1. *The Edit screen.*

Untitled instead.) Above and to the left of the filename are the four drop-down menus you use to issue commands to Edit. For this example, we will use only a couple of menu commands. (For information about any aspect of Edit, press F1 to access Edit's online help system.)

To create SHORTDIR.BAT, type the following commands, pressing Enter at the end of each line:

```
CLS
DIR /W
```

If you make a typing mistake, use the Backspace key to erase the error, and then retype the rest of the line. If the cursor is on another line, use the arrow keys to move the cursor to the line containing the error, and then use the Backspace key to correct the problem.

To save SHORTDIR.BAT on disk, open the File menu by first pressing the Alt key and then pressing the F key. Next choose the File menu's Save command by pressing S. (If you did not specify a filename when you started Edit, Edit displays a dialog box that asks you to enter the name of the file. Simply type *SHORTDIR.BAT*, and press Enter to name and save the file.)

NOTE: *If you have a mouse, you can easily access the commands in Edit's menus. Position the mouse pointer over the name of the menu, and click the left mouse button to open the menu. Then click the command you want to choose. For example, to save a file, click the File menu, and then click the Save command.*

Before you can try out the batch file, you must quit the Edit program, and return to the command prompt. To do this, press Alt, F (to open the File menu), and then X (to choose the File menu's Exit command).

To run your newly created batch file, type *SHORTDIR*:

```
C:\> SHORTDIR
```

Then press Enter. MS-DOS clears the screen and displays your directory listing with the filename's columns across the screen (as directed by the /W switch).

Edit also allows you to change an existing file. Let's change the SHORTDIR.BAT file so that MS-DOS displays only the files with the EXE extension. As before, type *EDIT*, and specify the filename:

```
C:\> EDIT SHORTDIR.BAT
```

Because the file already exists, Edit displays the contents of the file in its window, exactly as you typed it.

To change the file, you simply move the cursor to the line you want to change, make the change, and then save the file again. You want to add the *.EXE file filter to the second line, so begin by pressing the down-arrow key to move the cursor down one line. Then press the End key to move the cursor to the end of the line. Next press the left-arrow key two times to move the cursor under the /. (If you have a mouse, you can simply click the /.) Finally type *.*EXE* followed by one space. The /W already in the line moves to the right as you type, and the result looks something like Figure 1-2. (If your batch file differs from Figure 1-2, make any necessary corrections now.)

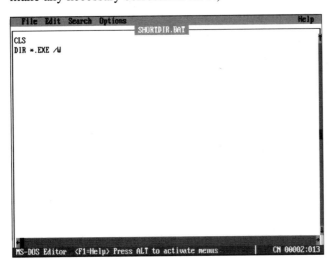

FIGURE 1-2. *SHORTDIR.BAT after editing.*

To save the changed file, press Alt, F, and then S. Finally, to quit the Edit program and return to the command prompt, press Alt, F, and then X. Now if you run the batch file, MS-DOS clears the screen and displays only the files with the EXE extension.

If you want to stop editing a file in Edit and return to the command prompt without saving any changes to the file, choose the File menu's Exit command. When you use the Exit command without saving a new file or the changes you made to an existing file, Edit displays the dialog box shown in Figure 1-3 on the following page to prevent you from accidentally quitting before saving any changes.

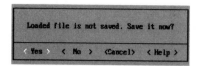

FIGURE 1-3. *The Exit dialog box.*

If you select Yes by pressing Enter, Edit saves any changes you made
to the file before it returns you to the command prompt. If you select
No by pressing the Tab key once and then pressing Enter, Edit does *not*
save any changes you made and returns you to the command prompt. If
you select Cancel by pressing the Esc key, Edit cancels the Exit command and returns you to the file, allowing you to continue the editing
session.

NOTE: *Unlike many other text editors, Edit does not make a backup copy of
the file's original contents when you edit a file and save changes. Instead,
the original contents are overwritten. As a rule, always use the COPY command to make a copy of important batch files yourself, before you change
their contents. Chapter 4 shows you how to create a batch file to perform
this task automatically.*

Creating a Batch File with Edlin

If you are working with MS-DOS version 4 or earlier, you can create
your batch files using Edlin. Edlin is a line editor (meaning you can
work with only one line at a time) that allows you to create and change
files. To understand how Edlin works, let's use it to create a batch file
named SHORTDIR.BAT that contains the CLS and DIR /W commands.

To begin, run Edlin from the command prompt, and specify the name
of the file you want to work with. (You must specify a filename in your
Edlin command line.) In this case, the following is your command line:

```
C:\> EDLIN SHORTDIR.BAT
```

When you press Enter, Edlin displays the following:

```
C:\> EDLIN SHORTDIR.BAT
New file
*
```

The asterisk symbol (∗) is the Edlin prompt. Edlin supports several single-letter commands. For this batch file, we will use only a few of these commands. (For a complete discussion of Edlin, refer to your MS-DOS user's manual.)

To insert a command in a batch file, you must issue the Edlin insert command, I, and press Enter:

```
C:\> EDLIN SHORTDIR.BAT
New file
*I
        1:*
```

Edlin prompts you to enter the first line of the batch file. Type *CLS*, and press Enter:

```
C:\> EDLIN SHORTDIR.BAT
New file
*I
        1:* CLS
        2:*
```

Edlin now prompts you for the second line. Type *DIR /W*, and press Enter:

```
C:\> EDLIN SHORTDIR.BAT
New file
*I
        1:* CLS
        2:* DIR /W
```

Because only two lines are required for this batch file, you must tell Edlin you've finished inserting text. To do this, hold down the Ctrl key, and press the C key. Then press Enter. When you press Ctrl-C, Edlin exits the insert mode and displays its prompt, as follows:

```
C:\> EDLIN SHORTDIR.BAT
New file
*I
        1:* CLS
        2:* DIR /W
        3:* ^C
*
```

To save the file, exit Edlin, and return to MS-DOS, enter the Edlin end command, E, and then press Enter. The result is shown on the following page.

```
C:\> EDLIN SHORTDIR.BAT
New file
*I
        1:* CLS
        2:* DIR /W
        3:* ^C
*E
```

```
C:\>
```

To run your newly created batch file, type *SHORTDIR*:

```
C:\> SHORTDIR
```

and press Enter. MS-DOS clears the screen and displays your directory listing with the filenames in columns across the screen (as directed by the /W switch).

As mentioned, Edlin also allows you to change an existing file. Let's change the SHORTDIR.BAT batch file so that MS-DOS displays only the files with the EXE extension. As before, type *EDLIN*, and specify the filename:

```
C:\> EDLIN SHORTDIR.BAT
```

Because the SHORTDIR.BAT file already exists, Edlin displays the following message:

```
C:\> EDLIN SHORTDIR.BAT
End of input file
*
```

In this case, Edlin is telling you that it has read the entire file and that it is ready to edit. Type the numeral *1* at the Edlin prompt, and press Enter. Edlin then displays the first line in the file:

```
C:\> EDLIN SHORTDIR.BAT
End of input file
*1
        1:* CLS
        1:*
```

The second 1:* that appears on your screen is Edlin's prompt for you to change line 1. If you want to leave line 1 unchanged, press Enter; otherwise, type the new text for line 1. For now, press Enter to leave line 1 unchanged:

```
C:\> EDLIN SHORTDIR.BAT
End of input file
*1
        1:* CLS
        1:*
*
```

At the Edlin prompt, type the numeral 2, and press Enter. Edlin displays the contents of line 2, allowing you to change them:

```
C:\> EDLIN SHORTDIR.BAT
End of input file
*1
        1:* CLS
        1:*
*2
        2:* DIR /W
        2:*
```

In this case, you need to change line 2 from DIR /W to DIR *.EXE /W. Type the new line, and press Enter:

```
C:\> EDLIN SHORTDIR.BAT
End of input file
*1
        1:* CLS
        1:*
*2
        2:* DIR /W
        2:* DIR *.EXE /W
*
```

Again, by entering the Edlin end command, E, and pressing Enter, you save the updated file contents and exit to MS-DOS:

```
C:\> EDLIN SHORTDIR.BAT
End of input file
*1
        1:* CLS
        1:*
*2
        2:* DIR /W
        2:* DIR *.EXE /W
*E

C:\>
```

If you now run the batch file, MS-DOS clears the screen and displays only the files with the EXE extension.

If you want to stop editing the file without saving any changes, use the Edlin quit command, Q. When you issue this command, Edlin responds with the following:

```
Abort edit (Y/N)?
```

If you type *Y* (for yes) and press Enter, Edlin ignores your edits, exits to MS-DOS, and leaves the file unchanged. If you type N (for no) and press Enter, Edlin continues the editing session.

Later in this book, we will use these editing techniques to create batch files that change your screen settings and assign commonly used MS-DOS commands to the function keys on your keyboard. We will also continue our discussion of MS-DOS batch files and batch-file commands.

CHAPTER 2

Setting the Stage

CUSTOMIZING YOUR SYSTEM WITH AUTOEXEC.BAT

Whether you know it or not, you use an MS-DOS batch file to customize your system. Each time your system starts, MS-DOS searches the root directory of the boot disk for a special file named AUTO-EXEC.BAT. If this batch file exists, MS-DOS executes the commands the file contains. If this batch file does not exist, MS-DOS executes the DATE and TIME commands instead.

In the past, you had to create your own AUTOEXEC.BAT file by following the steps for creating batch files presented in Chapter 1 of this book. When you install MS-DOS version 5 or later, however, the installation software creates an AUTOEXEC.BAT file for you. If you upgrade to MS-DOS version 5 or later from an earlier version, the installation software modifies your existing AUTOEXEC.BAT to ensure that it includes certain statements.

It's important to keep in mind that AUTOEXEC.BAT is an ordinary batch file whose contents you can change to meet your needs. However, because MS-DOS executes AUTOEXEC.BAT each time your system starts, you should thoroughly understand the effects of any changes you make to AUTOEXEC.BAT. If you're uncertain of the effects, you should hold off making any changes until you have read this book, particularly Chapter 12, which takes a detailed look at several commands you might want to include in your AUTOEXEC.BAT file.

Common AUTOEXEC.BAT Commands

To view the contents of your AUTOEXEC.BAT file, issue the following TYPE command:

```
C:\> TYPE \AUTOEXEC.BAT
```

Although your AUTOEXEC.BAT file probably contains several other commands, almost every AUTOEXEC.BAT file contains PATH and PROMPT commands similar to those shown here:

```
PATH C:\DOS
PROMPT $P$G
```

The installation programs of MS-DOS versions 5 and later make sure that these lines are in your AUTOEXEC.BAT file. If they are not, the programs add them.

The PATH command specifies the directories MS-DOS should search to locate external MS-DOS commands and other executable programs, such as batch files and application programs. The PATH command shown above tells MS-DOS to search the DOS directory on drive C. When you install a software program such as Windows, its installation program often updates the PATH command to include its directory. If you add Windows, the PATH command looks like this:

```
PATH C:\DOS;C:\WINDOWS
```

Note that the directory names specified in the PATH command are separated by semicolons (;). If you create a directory named BATCH in which to store your batch files, you can include the directory name in the search path, as shown here:

```
PATH C:\DOS;C:\WINDOWS;C:\BATCH
```

The PROMPT command shown at the top of the page uses the character $p to direct MS-DOS to display the current drive and directory in the command prompt and the character $g to display a greater than symbol (>). Chapter 12 examines the PROMPT command in detail. At that time, you will learn several ways to customize your command prompt.

Other Uses of AUTOEXEC.BAT

In addition to defining your search path and your command prompt, AUTOEXEC.BAT is often used to load memory-resident programs, such as DOSKEY, or to invoke graphical user interfaces, such as Windows or the MS-DOS Shell. As you read through Chapter 12, you will encounter several commands that you can put to use in your AUTO-EXEC.BAT file to instantly improve your system's performance.

CUSTOMIZING YOUR SYSTEM WITH CONFIG.SYS

During system startup, MS-DOS also executes the statements in a file called CONFIG.SYS. It does this work before it runs any of the commands in the AUTOEXEC.BAT file. Unlike AUTOEXEC.BAT, which contains the names of commands that MS-DOS executes, CONFIG.SYS contains entries that control how MS-DOS configures itself in memory. In addition, CONFIG.SYS lets you load device drivers (special software programs) that allow MS-DOS to support different hardware components, such as a mouse or CD-ROM. Do not confuse CONFIG.SYS and AUTOEXEC.BAT. Their only similarity is that MS-DOS uses them during system startup. The entries in CONFIG.SYS are not commands that you can type at the command prompt; they can be used only in CONFIG.SYS.

In the past, you had to create your own CONFIG.SYS file using an editor such as Edit. Beginning with MS-DOS version 5, the installation program creates a CONFIG.SYS file for you or makes changes to your existing file. To view the contents of your CONFIG.SYS file, issue the following TYPE command:

```
C:\> TYPE \CONFIG.SYS
```

The following table briefly describes several entries you can use in your CONFIG.SYS file:

Entry	Function
BREAK=	Enables/disables extended Ctrl-Break checking.
BUFFERS=	Specifies the number of disk I/O buffers.
COUNTRY=	Sets country-specific information. (Versions 2.1 and later)
DEVICE=	Installs a device driver in conventional memory (below 640 KB).
DEVICEHIGH=	Installs a device driver above 640 KB. (Versions 5 and later)
DOS=	Sets the area of RAM (above or below 640 KB) into which MS-DOS will load itself and enables the use of upper memory blocks. (Versions 5 and later)
DRIVPARM=	Specifies block device characteristics. (Versions 3.2 and later)

(continued)

(continued)

Entry	Function
FCBS=	Specifies the number of file control blocks MS-DOS supports for older programs. (Versions 3.0 and later)
FILES=	Specifies the number of files MS-DOS can have open at one time.
INCLUDE=	Includes one group of related startup entries within another. See Chapter 12. (Versions 6 and later)
INSTALL=	Allows loading of memory-resident programs (TSRs) during CONFIG.SYS processing. (Versions 4.0 and later)
LASTDRIVE=	Specifies the last drive letter that MS-DOS supports. (Versions 3.0 and later)
MENUCOLOR=	Specifies the color of the MS-DOS startup menu. See Chapter 12. (Versions 6 and later)
MENUDEFAULT=	Specifies a default option and time-out period for the MS-DOS startup menu. See Chapter 12. (Versions 6 and later)
MENUITEM=	Specifies an option that appears on the MS-DOS startup menu. See Chapter 12. (Versions 6 and later)
NUMLOCK=	Controls status of the NumLock key (and therefore the numeric keypad) at startup. (Versions 6 and later)
REM	Allows comment lines within a CONFIG.SYS file. (Versions 4.0 and later)
SET	Assigns a value to an MS-DOS environment variable. (Versions 6 and later)
SHELL=	Defines a command processor other than MS-DOS.
STACKS=	Provides additional stack space for systems encountering too many hardware interrupts at one time. (Versions 3.2 and later)
SUBMENU=	Defines a second level of menu options for the MS-DOS startup menu. See Chapter 12. (Versions 6 and later)
SWITCHES=	Controls the availability of the interactive startup and specifies conventional keyboard functions when an extended keyboard is installed. (Versions 5 and later)

If you are using MS-DOS version 6 or later, CONFIG.SYS supports several new and very powerful entries. Chapter 12 discusses these CONFIG.SYS entries in detail.

CHANGING AUTOEXEC.BAT AND CONFIG.SYS

As you work with MS-DOS, you will probably want to make changes to your AUTOEXEC.BAT and CONFIG.SYS files. As a precaution, do not make changes to these files until you have made copies of them. Then if your changes cause a startup error, you can always restore the original files. The following command, for example, copies the contents of AUTOEXEC.BAT to a file named AUTOEXEC.SAV:

```
C:\> COPY \AUTOEXEC.BAT \AUTOEXEC.SAV
```

Of course, the whole point of this book is to show you how to automate such tasks. In Chapter 4, we will write a batch file that creates a backup copy and then opens the Edit text editor—all with one command.

CHAPTER 3

Essential Batch-File Commands and Concepts

SUPPRESSING THE DISPLAY OF BATCH-FILE COMMAND NAMES

By default, when you execute a batch file, MS-DOS displays the name of each command as it executes. For example, let's look again at the GETINV.BAT batch file, which contains the CALCINV, SORTINV, PRINTINV, and ORDERINV commands. After you run the batch file, your screen looks as follows:

```
C:\> GETINV

C:\> CALCINV
...Calculating current product inventory

C:\> SORTINV
...Sorting inventory by quantity

C:\> PRINTINV
...Printing inventory

C:\> ORDERINV
...Generating purchase orders

C:\>
```

You might not always want MS-DOS to display the names of the batch-file commands as they execute. Your reason for suppressing the command-name display might simply be to reduce screen clutter, or you might not want a user of the batch file to know the commands that MS-DOS is executing. Depending on your version of MS-DOS, you can suppress command-name display in batch files in two ways.

With MS-DOS versions 3.3 and later, you can place the @ character at
the start of a command name to suppress the command-name display.
For example, the following batch file, VERVOL.BAT, displays the current MS-DOS version number as well as the current disk volume label,
but because both the VER and VOL batch-file commands are preceded
by the @ character, MS-DOS does not display the command name:

```
@VER
@VOL
```

When you run this batch file, MS-DOS displays the current MS-DOS
version and disk volume label, as follows:

```
MS-DOS version 6.20


 Volume in drive C is DOS 6 DISK
 Volume Serial Number is 3921-18D3

C:\>
```

Contrast this output with that of another batch file, VERVOL2.BAT,
whose VER and VOL commands do not suppress the command names.
When you run this batch file, MS-DOS displays the following:

```
C:\> VER

MS-DOS version 6.20

C:\> VOL

 Volume in drive C is DOS 6 DISK
 Volume Serial Number is 3921-18D3

C:\>
```

To suppress command-name display with earlier MS-DOS versions,
you must use the ECHO batch-file command. When the first batch-file
command is ECHO OFF, MS-DOS does not display the names of the
batch-file commands as they execute. For example, the following batch
file, VERVOL3.BAT, uses ECHO OFF:

```
ECHO OFF
VER
VOL
```

When you run this batch file, MS-DOS displays the lines shown on the
following page.

```
C:\> ECHO OFF

MS-DOS version 3.2

 Volume in drive C is DOS_DISK
 Volume Serial Number is 3921-18D3

C:\>
```

As you can see, MS-DOS does not display the VER and VOL command names. However, MS-DOS does display this message:

```
C:\> ECHO OFF
```

With MS-DOS version 3.3 or later, you can suppress the ECHO OFF message by preceding the ECHO OFF command with the @ character.

If you are using a version of MS-DOS earlier than 3.3, consider placing the CLS command in the batch file immediately following the ECHO

ECHO Batch-File Command

Function:

Suppresses or enables the display of command names as MS-DOS executes the commands within a batch file.

Format:

ECHO ON

or

ECHO OFF

Notes:

The ECHO OFF command suppresses the display of command names within a batch file as MS-DOS executes each command. By suppressing the display of command names, you reduce screen clutter and reduce the possibility of confusing users. By default, MS-DOS uses ECHO ON, displaying each command name as the command executes. MS-DOS resets ECHO to ON at the end of a batch file. If you are using MS-DOS version 3.3 or later, you can suppress command names in a batch file by preceding each name with the @ character. With earlier versions, you can use the CLS command to clear the screen after turning off ECHO.

In addition to enabling and disabling command-name display, the ECHO batch-file command lets your batch files display messages.

OFF command to clear the screen before displaying the output of the
VER and VOL commands, as shown here:

```
ECHO OFF
CLS
VER
VOL
```

Let's assume that this batch file is named VERVOL4.BAT. When you
run the file, MS-DOS displays the ECHO OFF message, clears the
screen, and then displays the following:

```
MS-DOS version 6.20

 Volume in drive C is DOS 6 DISK
 Volume Serial Number is 3921-18D3

C:\>
```

Example:

Assume that your batch file contains the TIME and DATE commands,
as follows:

```
TIME
DATE
```

When you run the batch file, MS-DOS (by default) displays each command name as the command executes:

```
C:\> TIME
Current time is 11:26:46.03a
Enter new time:

C:\> DATE
Current date is Thu 04-07-1994
Enter new date (mm-dd-yy):
```

You could add the @ECHO OFF command to your batch file, as follows:

```
@ECHO OFF
TIME
DATE
```

When you run the batch file, MS-DOS suppresses the command-name
display as the batch file executes, and then displays the following:

```
Current time is 11:26:46.03a
Enter new time:
Current date is Thu 04-07-1994
Enter new date (mm-dd-yy):
```

Later in this chapter, we will use the ECHO command extensively in batch files to write messages to the user. In Chapter 8, we'll use ECHO to set the screen colors and redefine keys on the keyboard. For now, however, understand that the ECHO OFF command inhibits the display of batch-file commands when MS-DOS executes a batch file.

If you want to display the names of some commands as they execute (you will see why you might want to do this later), you can use the ECHO ON command (the MS-DOS default setting). The following batch file, VERVOL5.BAT, illustrates how you might use ECHO ON and ECHO OFF:

```
ECHO OFF
CLS
VER
ECHO ON
VOL
```

When you run this batch file, MS-DOS displays the following:

```
MS-DOS version 6.20


C:\> VOL

  Volume in drive C is DOS 6 DISK
  Volume Serial Number is 3921-18D3

C:\>
```

As you can see, MS-DOS suppresses the display of the CLS, VER, and ECHO ON command names. After the ECHO ON command completes execution, MS-DOS enables the command-name display, displaying the VOL command name.

NOTE: *Many users prefer to precede the commands in AUTOEXEC.BAT with the @ character or the ECHO OFF command. Either method suppresses the display of command names as MS-DOS executes the commands in AUTOEXEC.BAT.*

INTERRUPTING A BATCH FILE

If at any time you need to interrupt the execution of the commands in a batch file, you can hold down the Ctrl key and press C. When MS-DOS detects that you have pressed Ctrl-C, it displays ^C and the following message:

```
Terminate batch job (Y/N)?
```

If you press Y, MS-DOS immediately stops processing the batch file. If you press N, MS-DOS ends the command it is currently executing, continuing execution with the next command in the batch file.

To better understand this process, let's reexamine the TIMEDATE.BAT batch file, which contains the TIME and DATE commands. When you run this batch file, MS-DOS first executes the TIME command, as follows:

```
C:\> TIMEDATE
Current time is 11:39:22.25a
Enter new time:
```

If instead of entering a new time, you press Ctrl-C, MS-DOS asks you whether you want to end the batch file, as follows:

```
C:\> TIMEDATE
Current time is 11:39:22.25a
Enter new time: ^C

Terminate batch job (Y/N)?
```

In this case, press Y. MS-DOS ends the execution of the entire batch file, immediately returning control to the command prompt.

Run TIMEDATE.BAT a second time, and again press Ctrl-C at the TIME prompt:

```
C:\> TIMEDATE
Current time is 11:39:22.25a
Enter new time: ^C

Terminate batch job (Y/N)?
```

This time, press N. Instead of ending the batch file, MS-DOS ends only the current command, continuing execution with the next command in the batch file, which in this case is DATE:

```
C:\> TIMEDATE
Current time is 11:39:22.25a
Enter new time: ^C

Terminate batch job (Y/N)? N
Current date is Thu 04-07-1994
Enter new date (mm-dd-yy):
```

REDIRECTING A BATCH FILE'S OUTPUT

When you execute a batch file by typing its name at the command prompt, you cannot use I/O redirection to send the output of the batch file somewhere other than the screen. However, you can use I/O direction *within* a batch file. For example, the DIRAB.BAT batch file consists of the following:

```
DIR A:*.*
DIR B:*.*
```

You can try executing the batch file by typing the following:

```
DIRAB > DIRAB.OUT
```

However, the output of the DIR commands within the batch file will *not* be directed to the file DIRAB.OUT. To direct the DIR output to a file, you must include I/O redirection on a specific MS-DOS command line within the batch file. In other words, you need to rewrite DIRAB.BAT as follows:

```
DIR A:*.* > DIRAB.OUT
DIR B:*.* >> DIRAB.OUT
```

When you run the revised DIRAB.BAT, MS-DOS redirects the output of both DIR commands to the file. The single > creates a new file. The double >> appends the information to the existing file.

This batch file displays both DIR command lines on the screen as they execute. To suppress the command-name display, use the ECHO OFF command or use the @ character as follows:

```
@DIR A:*.* > DIRAB.OUT
@DIR B:*.* >> DIRAB.OUT
```

HELPING OTHERS UNDERSTAND YOUR BATCH FILES

The name you give a batch file should hint at the batch file's overall purpose. As your batch files increase in complexity, however, you might have difficulty remembering not only the batch file's sequence of commands but also the switches each command line uses. To help you remember, or to help another user who is reading the file understand what the batch file does, MS-DOS provides the REM batch-file command. REM (for Remark) allows you to place remarks, or comments, in your batch files. When MS-DOS encounters REM, it continues execution with the next command in the batch file.

Consider how the REM command improves the readability of the GETINV.BAT batch file:

```
@ECHO OFF
REM   Name: GETINV.BAT
REM   Function: Executes the commands for
REM   inventory processing.
REM
REM   Written By: K. Jamsa 4/01/93
REM
REM   Use the CALCINV program to determine
REM   the current inventory status.
CALCINV
REM   Use the SORTINV program to generate
REM   a sorted listing of the current inventory.
SORTINV
REM   Use the PRINTINV program to print
REM   hard copies of the current inventory.
PRINTINV
REM   Use the ORDERINV program to
REM   initiate inventory purchase orders.
ORDERINV
```

At first glance, the length of the batch file might be intimidating. However, after you read the remarks, the operation of the batch file becomes clear.

The first command, @ECHO OFF, disables the display of MS-DOS command names as the batch file executes (without displaying the ECHO command). If you don't include the ECHO OFF command, MS-DOS displays each REM command on the screen as the batch file executes. (REM is meant to help people who *read* your batch files, but displaying REM commands on the screen can confuse the user.)

Next lines 2 through 6 explain the purpose of the batch file, who wrote it, and when it was written. Including the author's name gives users a person to contact about the batch file, and including the creation date allows you to determine whether you are using the most recent version of the batch file.

If someone else changes the batch file, that person should add a remark like the one on the following page to document the date and reason for the change.

```
@ECHO OFF
REM  Name: GETINV.BAT
REM  Function:  Executes the commands for
REM  inventory processing.
REM
REM  Written by: K. Jamsa 4/01/94
REM  Last change: D. Jamsa 4/12/93 Print two
REM  inventory copies.
REM
```

Even the simplest batch file can be confusing several weeks after you
create it. To reduce the potential for confusion, use REM extensively in
your batch files. The few minutes you spend documenting a batch file
today will save you much time and effort should you need to change
the batch file later.

REM Batch-File Command

Function:

Allows you to place remarks in a batch file to explain the batch file's
operation.

Format:

REM text

Notes:

As a batch file's complexity increases, so does the difficulty of understanding the batch file's processing. The REM batch-file command lets
you place remarks in a batch file that explain its purpose. When MS-
DOS encounters a REM command, it ignores the command, continuing
execution of the batch file with the command on the next line.

The ECHO OFF command suppresses the display of remarks.

Example:

You might want to include several lines at the top of your batch
files that explain who wrote the batch file and when it was written,
as follows:

```
REM Monthly backup procedures.
REM Written by: K. Jamsa
REM            04/01/1993
REM Function: Performs a complete disk backup of
REM           all the files on your disk.
```

RUNNING YOUR BATCH FILES
ONE COMMAND AT A TIME

MS-DOS version 6.2 offers a way to run your batch files one command at a time. If you have a complex batch file that isn't working as you would like, you can step through the file and find out which command is giving you the problem. You can also choose to skip any command.

To step through a batch file, use the COMMAND command with the /Y and /C switches and the name of the file. MS-DOS verifies that you want to run the batch file and then stops at each command in the batch file, prompting you to run the command by typing Y, or skip the command by typing N. The following example shows how to use COMMAND to step through the TIMEDATE batch file. It skips the TIME command and runs the DATE comand:

```
C:\> COMMAND /Y /C TIMEDATE
TIMEDATE[Y/N]?Y

C:\> TIME
TIME[Y/N]?N
C:\> DATE
DATE[Y/N]?Y
Current date is Thu 04-07-1994
Enter new date (mm-dd-yy):

C:\>
```

TEMPORARILY SUSPENDING BATCH-FILE PROCESSING

Many batch files execute all their commands—from the first to the last—without user intervention. For those times when your batch file needs to wait until you place a printer on line or insert a floppy disk in a drive, you can use the PAUSE batch-file command to display a message, suspending batch-file processing until you press a key to continue.

When the PAUSE command executes, it displays the message specified in its command line, followed by this line:

```
Press any key to continue . . .
```

When you press any key, the batch file resumes processing with the next command. (To end the batch file's processing at the PAUSE prompt, press Ctrl-C.)

For example, a batch file named PRINTDIR.BAT that prints the files in the current directory might display the following message before printing the directory listing:

```
PAUSE Place the printer on line
Press any key to continue . . .
```

This batch file contains the following two commands:

```
PAUSE Place the printer on line
DIR > PRN
```

When you execute this batch file, PAUSE waits for you to press any key before continuing with the DIR command on the next line. The > PRN directs the output to the printer as an ASCII text file.

Another batch file, PAUSETWO.BAT, might use the PAUSE command twice to obtain a printed listing of the files in drive A. The first PAUSE tells you to place a disk in drive A, and the second PAUSE tells you to place the printer on line, as follows:

```
PAUSE Put disk with directory to print in drive A
PAUSE Place the printer on line
DIR A: > PRN
```

When you run this batch file, MS-DOS executes the first PAUSE command and displays the following:

```
PAUSE Put disk with directory to print in drive A
Press any key to continue . . .
```

When you place a disk in drive A and press a key, the batch file executes the second PAUSE command and displays the following:

```
PAUSE Place the printer on line
Press any key to continue . . .
```

When you place the printer on line and press a key, the batch file executes the DIR command, redirecting the directory output to the printer as instructed.

Notice that neither of the preceding two batch files used the ECHO OFF command to suppress the display of batch-file command names.

Including an ECHO OFF command suppresses the message specified on the PAUSE command line, so that the only output is this message:

```
Press any key to continue . . .
```

For example, the following batch file, NOMSG.BAT, illustrates this undesirable result:

```
ECHO OFF
PAUSE Place the printer on line
DIR > PRN
```

When you run this batch file, MS-DOS displays the following:

```
C:\> ECHO OFF
Press any key to continue . . .
```

MS-DOS suppresses the message *Place the printer on line.*

A batch file that uses the PAUSE command is very likely to use both the ECHO ON and ECHO OFF commands to display some batch-file command names and suppress others. Consider this batch file, named ECHOTEST.BAT, which enables and disables command-name display so that the PAUSE message is not suppressed:

```
ECHO OFF
VER
VOL
ECHO ON
PAUSE Just turned ECHO ON
ECHO OFF
VER
VOL
```

When you run this batch file, MS-DOS displays the following:

```
C:\> ECHO OFF

MS-DOS version 6.20


    Volume in drive C is DOS 6 DISK
    Volume Serial Number is 3921-18D3

C:\> PAUSE Just turned ECHO ON
Press any key to continue . . .

C:\> ECHO OFF
```

(continued)

```
MS-DOS version 6.20


Volume in drive C is DOS 6 DISK
Volume Serial Number is 3921-18D3

C:\>
```

Remember, if you are using MS-DOS version 3.3 or later, you can suppress the ECHO OFF message by putting an @ character at the beginning of the ECHO OFF command line.

Getting the User's Attention with PAUSE

Depending on the number of commands in a batch file and on how long it takes to run, you might start a batch file and leave it unattended while working on other tasks away from the computer. If the batch file executes a PAUSE command, a considerable amount of time might pass before you press a key to continue batch-file processing.

Rather than using PAUSE to simply display a message, you might want the command to also generate the bell sound on your computer's built-in speaker. As you will see, when you know a bit about the ASCII character set that the computer uses to display letters, numbers, and symbols on your screen, generating the computer's bell sound is easy.

Each character that the computer displays or that your printer prints is represented by a unique value. The ASCII character set consists of 128 values from 0 through 127 that include the uppercase and lowercase letters of the alphabet, the digits from 0 through 9, and common punctuation symbols, as well as special values that have unique meaning to the computer. The ASCII value 7, for example, directs the computer to send the bell sound to its built-in speaker. (In Chapter 8, we will use a set of values from 128 through 255, called the *IBM extended character set*, that allows the IBM PC and PC compatibles to display boxes and mathematical characters.)

For the PAUSE command to sound your computer's bell, the message in the PAUSE command line must contain the ASCII 7 character. Three methods are available for placing this character in the PAUSE command line.

Let's begin by creating a batch file named BELL.BAT by copying the file from the keyboard, as follows:

```
C:\> COPY CON BELL.BAT
```

Type the word *PAUSE* followed by a space, but don't press Enter. Next enter an ASCII 7 character in the PAUSE command line by holding down the Alt key and pressing the 7 key on your numeric keypad. (Note: You must use the numeric keypad—not the row of number keys across the top of your keyboard.) When you release the Alt key, MS-DOS displays the characters *^G* (pronounced *Control G*) on your screen, as follows:

```
C:\> COPY CON BELL.BAT
PAUSE ^G
```

Press the Alt-7 key combination two more times. (The Alt key must be released between successive entries of ASCII values.)

```
C:\> COPY CON BELL.BAT
PAUSE ^G^G^G
```

Next complete the batch file by entering the message *BELL BELL BELL* and pressing F6, as follows:

```
C:\> COPY CON BELL.BAT
PAUSE ^G^G^GBELL BELL BELL
^Z
        1 File(s) copied

C:\>
```

When you run the batch file, MS-DOS displays *PAUSE,* sounds your computer's bell three times, displays the message *BELL BELL BELL* followed by *Press any key to continue . . .* (on a separate line), and awaits your response.

MS-DOS represents the ASCII 7 character on your screen with the special character *^G*. The second method of entering the ASCII character that sounds your computer's bell uses the Ctrl-G key combination. As before, create the BELL.BAT batch file by copying it from the keyboard. (Doing so overwrites the previous version of the file on disk.) Type the word *PAUSE,* followed by a space:

```
C:\> COPY CON BELL.BAT
PAUSE
```

Next press Ctrl-G. MS-DOS displays the lines on the following page.

```
C:\> COPY CON BELL.BAT
PAUSE ^G
```

Repeat the Ctrl-G process twice, and then type the word *BELL* three times, creating the following batch file:

```
C:\> COPY CON BELL.BAT
PAUSE ^G^G^GBELL BELL BELL
^Z
      1 File(s) copied
```

```
C:\>
```

When you run this batch file, MS-DOS displays *PAUSE,* sounds your computer's bell three times, displays the words *BELL BELL BELL* on your screen, moves to a new line, displays the message *Press any key to continue . . .* , and awaits your response.

The third technique for creating a file containing the bell character is to use Edit. To create the file BELL2.BAT, start Edit as follows:

```
C:\> EDIT BELL2.BAT
```

Begin by typing the word *PAUSE* followed by a space.

PAUSE Batch-File Command

Function:

Temporarily suspends the processing of a batch file after displaying an optional message. When the user presses any key, batch-file processing continues.

Format:

  PAUSE [message]

Notes:

When your batch file executes PAUSE, MS-DOS displays the optional message in the PAUSE command line, followed by this message:

```
Press any key to continue . . .
```

If the user presses any key, batch-file processing continues with the next command in the batch file. If the user does not want to continue batch-file processing, the user can end the batch file by pressing Ctrl-C and then pressing Y to respond to the message *Terminate batch job (Y/N)?*

Characters such as ^G are often referred to as control characters because they are used to control the processing of programs. If you simply press Ctrl-G while working within Edit, nothing happens. If you want to insert a control character in your text, you must first instruct Edit to treat the character as an entry rather than as a command. You do this with the Ctrl-P command. Ctrl-P instructs Edit to insert the next character exactly as it is typed rather than trying to interpret it as a command.

To enter the ^G character, press Ctrl-P, Ctrl-G. You can either hold down the Ctrl key, press the letter P, release the Ctrl key, hold down the Ctrl key again, and press the G key, or you can hold down the Ctrl key, press the P key, and, keeping the Ctrl key down, press the G key. The advantage of the first method is that it emphasizes that you are entering two distinct character combinations, Ctrl-P and Ctrl-G. The advantage of the second method is that it is easier.

Using the second method, hold down the Ctrl key and press the P and G keys (in that order). When you do this, you see the screen shown in Figure 3-1 on the following page.

The ECHO OFF batch-file command suppresses the display of the optional message specified in the PAUSE command line. If your batch file specifies ECHO OFF, the PAUSE command still displays the message *Press any key to continue . . .* and suspends batch-file processing until the user presses a key.

Example:

The following batch file prompts the user to insert a floppy disk containing an application called PAYROLL in drive A and press any key to continue:

```
PAUSE Insert PAYROLL disk in drive A
A:PAYROLL
```

When you run this batch file, MS-DOS displays the following:

```
C:\> PAUSE Insert PAYROLL disk in drive A
Press any key to continue . . .
```

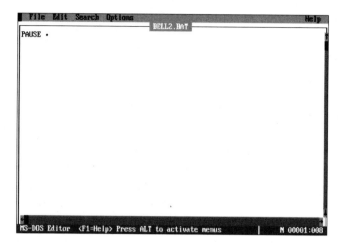

FIGURE 3-1. *The screen representation of a control character (the small dot).*

Edit displays the small dot to represent control characters. To complete the batch file, enter two more Ctrl-G characters followed by the words *BELL BELL BELL*. (You must use Ctrl-P before each of the Ctrl-G characters. You can hold down the Ctrl key and press P, G, P, G.) When you are finished, your screen should look like the one shown in Figure 3-2.

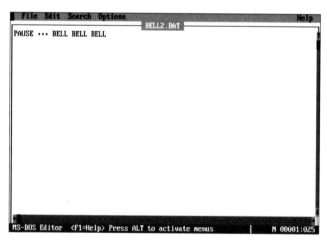

FIGURE 3-2. *The complete attention-getting command line.*

To save the new batch file with the existing name (BELL2.BAT), select the File menu, and choose the Save command (Alt-F,S). Finally, to return to the command prompt, select the File menu, and then choose the Exit command (Alt-F,X).

When you run this batch file (by typing BELL2 at the prompt), MS-DOS displays the word *PAUSE*, sounds your computer's bell three times, displays the words *BELL BELL BELL* on your screen, moves to a new line, displays *Press any key to continue . . .* , and awaits your response.

NOTE: *With versions of MS-DOS earlier than 5, you will need to use Edlin rather than Edit. In Edlin, you can enter any control character directly by typing it as you did in the second COPY CON example.*

NOTE: *If you usually create batch files with a word processor, refer to the word processor's documentation to find out how to enter ASCII characters.*

DISPLAYING MESSAGES WITH THE ECHO COMMAND

The PAUSE command allows a batch file to display a message to the user. However, after each message that PAUSE displays, the user must press a key to continue. You might want your batch files to display messages or prompts that don't require the user to press a key. In such instances, the ECHO batch-file command provides a solution. In addition to enabling and disabling command-name display, ECHO lets batch files display a single-line message. Before using ECHO to display messages, most batch files first suppress command-name display by using the ECHO OFF command. For example, a batch file named MESSAGE.BAT displays the following messages:

```
First Message
Second Message
Third Message
```

This batch file's commands are:

```
@ECHO OFF
ECHO First Message
ECHO Second Message
ECHO Third Message
```

The batch file first disables command-name display by using ECHO OFF. Without this ECHO OFF command, the batch-file output is somewhat cluttered, as you can see on the following page.

```
C:\> ECHO First Message
First Message

C:\> ECHO Second Message
Second Message

C:\> ECHO Third Message
Third Message
```

The ECHO command's message-display capability has many uses, ranging from displaying batch-file menus to setting screen colors to redefining keys on your keyboard (with the latter two using the ANSI.SYS device driver). Notice how the ECHO command displays copyright information in the following batch file:

```
@ECHO OFF
REM   Name: GETINV.BAT
REM   Function: Executes the commands for
REM   inventory processing.
REM
REM   Written by: K. Jamsa 4/01/93
REM
REM   Display copyright information.
ECHO GETINV.BAT (Copyright 1993. KAJ Software)
ECHO All rights reserved.

REM   Use the CALCINV program to determine
REM   the current inventory status.
CALCINV

REM   Use the SORTINV program to generate
REM   a sorted listing of the current inventory.
SORTINV

REM   Use the PRINTINV program to print
REM   hard copies of the current inventory.
PRINTINV

REM   Use the ORDERINV program to
REM   initiate inventory purchase orders.
ORDERINV
```

When you run this batch file, MS-DOS first displays:

```
GETINV.BAT (Copyright 1994. KAJ Software)
All rights reserved.
```

As you can see, ECHO allows you to display meaningful messages to the user without interrupting the batch file's processing.

Combining ECHO and PAUSE

Sometimes you want to display a specific message and then give the user a chance to respond. You might want to provide the user with more than the standard *Press any key to continue . . .* message or you might want to replace that message entirely. You can accomplish this feat by using an ECHO batch-file command followed by a PAUSE command.

The following batch file, MYTEXT.BAT, uses this technique to provide the user with more information than the standard PAUSE message:

```
@ECHO OFF
ECHO Press Ctrl-C to cancel execution or
PAUSE
```

When this file is run, MS-DOS displays the following:

```
Press Ctrl-C to cancel execution or
Press any key to continue . . .
```

MS-DOS then waits for the user to respond. The first line, @ECHO OFF, suppresses the display of the batch-file commands. The second line displays additional information about the user's options. The third and final line displays the standard PAUSE message and then causes the processing of the batch file to stop until the user responds.

With this technique, you gain greater control over the display of messages within your batch file. These lines can be incorporated into any batch file where you want to give the user information about the options available at a PAUSE command (Ctrl-C to stop or any other key to continue).

You might want to suppress the message generated by the PAUSE command completely. To do this, you must redirect the output to the NUL device. The following batch file, MYTEXT2.BAT, completely replaces the PAUSE message with one from an ECHO command:

```
@ECHO OFF
ECHO Press any key other than Ctrl-C to continue . . .
PAUSE > NUL
```

This batch file displays the message from the ECHO command and then pauses. The standard *Press any key to continue . . .* message is redirected to the NUL device and does not appear. (The NUL device is often referred to as a *bit bucket* and is extremely useful for disposing of unwanted output.)

ECHO Message Batch-File Command

Function:

Displays a single-line message.

Format:

ECHO message

Notes:

In addition to enabling and disabling command-name display within your batch files, the ECHO batch-file command also lets your batch files display single-line messages. The message can be as simple as a single line of text that tells the user a file was not found, or it can contain ANSI escape sequences that clear the screen and set screen colors. As examples, in this book you will use ECHO to draw menus, sound your computer's bell, and redefine keys on your keyboard.

If you are using MS-DOS version 5 or later, you can direct ECHO to display a blank line by following ECHO with a period, as follows:

```
ECHO.
```

If you are using a version of MS-DOS earlier than 5, you can direct ECHO to display a blank line by following ECHO with the IBM extended character created by the Alt-255 keyboard combination.

Example:

This batch file uses ECHO to sound the computer's bell, telling the user that inventory processing is finished:

```
ECHO OFF
CALCINV
SORTINV
PRINTINV
ORDERINV
ECHO ^G^G^GInventory processing is complete
ECHO Inventory status information is printing
```

Remember, pressing Ctrl-G displays ^G at the command prompt. Press Ctrl-P and then Ctrl-G to insert the bell sound in Edit. When this batch file completes execution, your computer's bell sounds three times, and MS-DOS displays the following:

```
Inventory processing is complete
Inventory status information is printing
```

Adding Blank Lines

Sometimes you might want your messages to include blank lines. By default, if you execute ECHO with no command-line parameter (such as the word *ON* or *OFF,* or a message), ECHO displays its current status: ECHO ON or ECHO OFF. For example, if you enter the ECHO command at the command prompt, you'll see the following:

```
C:\> ECHO
ECHO is on

C:\>
```

The following batch file, named SHOWECHO.BAT, calls ECHO to display its current status throughout the batch file's processing:

```
@ECHO Displaying default state
@ECHO
@ECHO Turning ECHO OFF
@ECHO OFF
@ECHO
```

When you run this batch file, MS-DOS displays this:

```
C:\> SHOWECHO
Displaying default state
ECHO is on
Turning ECHO OFF
ECHO is off
```

Even if you place several space characters after the ECHO command, ECHO still displays its current status. MS-DOS version 5 or later lets you display a blank line by entering the ECHO command immediately followed by a period (ECHO.). For example, the following batch file displays three blank lines:

```
@ECHO OFF
ECHO Start
ECHO.
ECHO.
ECHO.
ECHO Done
```

For versions of MS-DOS earlier than 5, the secret to displaying a blank line using ECHO lies in the IBM extended character value 255. The ASCII character set uses the value 32 for the blank character you enter by pressing the keyboard's spacebar. If the ECHO command line contains only this type of blank character, ECHO displays its status. As it turns out, the IBM extended character value 255 also represents a blank character. However, the ECHO command does not recognize this value as a blank, so placing the IBM extended character value 255 in the ECHO command line displays a blank line as you intended.

To demonstrate, create a batch file named BLANK.BAT by copying the commands from the keyboard:

```
C:\> COPY CON BLANK.BAT
```

Begin the batch file by setting ECHO OFF and clearing the screen:

```
ECHO OFF
CLS
ECHO Skip one line
```

Next, to skip a line, type the word *ECHO* followed by a space, and hold down the Alt key while typing *255* on the numeric keypad. When you release the Alt key, the cursor moves one character position to the right, and the ECHO command line now contains the IBM extended character value 255.

Use the same procedure to complete the batch file:

```
C:\> COPY CON BLANK.BAT
ECHO OFF
CLS
ECHO Skip one line
ECHO <Alt-255 here>
ECHO Skip two lines
ECHO <Alt-255 here>
ECHO <Alt-255 here>
ECHO Last line
^Z
        1 File(s) copied

C:\>
```

When you run this batch file, MS-DOS displays the following:

```
Skip one line

Skip two lines


Last line
```

If ECHO displays its current status when you run the batch file, you have not correctly entered the Alt-255 key combination for the three

ECHO commands that are supposed to produce blank lines. (Remember, you must use the numeric keypad.)

If you use Edlin to create a batch file that displays a blank line, you can hold down the Alt key and type *255* (using the numeric keypad) to produce the required blank character.

As you can see, displaying a blank line with the ECHO. command is easier than using Alt-255.

WHERE TO STORE YOUR BATCH FILES ON DISK

Many people initially place their batch files in the same directory as the MS-DOS external commands because that directory is usually defined as part of the search path by the PATH= entry in their AUTO-EXEC.BAT file. A better strategy is to create a unique directory for the batch files you use frequently. You can create a directory named BATCH with this command line:

```
C:\> MKDIR \BATCH
```

After you copy your batch files to this directory, you can modify the PATH statement in your AUTOEXEC.BAT file to add the directory to your search path. The following PATH command, for example, includes both the BATCH directory and the DOS directory on the search path:

```
PATH C:\DOS;C:\BATCH
```

If you add your batch-files directory to your search path, keep in mind that MS-DOS might have to examine every filename in the directory when it searches for your batch file. If the directory contains several seldom-used batch files, the time spent examining their filenames is wasted, so store only frequently used batch files in this directory.

NOTE: *You can reverse the order, as in the following:*

```
PATH C:\BATCH;C:\DOS
```

Batch files with the same name as external commands are then used instead of the MS-DOS commands.

CHAPTER 4

Using Parameters to Increase Batch-File Flexibility

GETTING STARTED WITH BATCH-FILE PARAMETERS

Batch files exist to save you time and keystrokes. Let's look at a batch file named P.BAT that prints a copy of your AUTOEXEC.BAT file. The batch file is very short, containing only the following command:

```
PRINT \AUTOEXEC.BAT
```

When you want to print the contents of your AUTOEXEC.BAT file, you can simply press P and then press Enter.

Although P.BAT saves you several keystrokes, it isn't very functional because you can use it to print the contents of only one specific file. A more flexible batch file would print the contents of *any* file.

When you type a command at the command prompt, the command line often consists of two parts: a command name such as DISKCOPY and command-line parameters such as the disk-drive identifiers A: and B: shown here:

```
C:\> DISKCOPY A: B:
```

Command   Command-line parameters

You can also use parameters in batch files. For example, you can quickly create a P.BAT batch file that prints any file, by modifying the batch file like this:

```
PRINT %1
```

The batch file still contains the PRINT command, but now the command directs MS-DOS to print %1 instead of AUTOEXEC.BAT. You run the batch file by typing *P* followed by a filename, like this:

```
C:\> P \AUTOEXEC.BAT
```

MS-DOS then assigns the first command-line parameter—in this case, \AUTOEXEC.BAT—to the %1 variable, as follows:

```
C:\> P \AUTOEXEC.BAT

    PRINT %1

    PRINT \AUTOEXEC.BAT
```

You can later run the batch file with the following command line:

```
C:\> P \CONFIG.SYS
```

MS-DOS then assigns \CONFIG.SYS to %1, as follows:

```
C:\> P \CONFIG.SYS

    PRINT %1

    PRINT \CONFIG.SYS
```

In a similar way, you can create a batch file named VIEWIT.BAT that uses the following command to let you view the contents of a specific file one screenful at a time:

```
TYPE %1 ¦ MORE
```

Assuming that you invoke the batch file with the CONFIG.SYS filename, the batch file would perform the following parameter substitution:

```
C:\> VIEWIT \CONFIG.SYS

      TYPE %1 ¦ MORE

      TYPE \CONFIG.SYS ¦ MORE
```

You have greatly increased the flexibility of the batch file by using one batch-file parameter. To enhance your processing capabilities to an even greater extent, MS-DOS supports the batch-file parameters %0 through %9. (Each time you run a batch file, MS-DOS assigns the name of the batch file to the %0 variable.) As you just learned, MS-DOS assigns the first command-line parameter to the %1 variable. If your batch-file command line contains several parameters, such as the following, MS-DOS assigns the parameters to consecutive variables, starting with %1 and continuing through %9 (if that many exist):

```
C:\> PAYROLL JUNE JULY AUGUST
```

In this case the assignments become the following:

The following batch file, SHOWNAME.BAT, uses the ECHO batch-file command to display its own name:

```
@ECHO OFF
ECHO %0
```

When you run this batch file, MS-DOS displays this:

```
SHOWNAME
```

Using Batch-File Parameters

Each time you run a batch file, MS-DOS assigns the components of the batch file's command line (including the batch-file name and any parameters) to variables. MS-DOS lets your batch files access up to nine parameters using the variables %1 through %9. For example, the following command line runs the SHOWIT.BAT batch file, passing the AUTOEXEC.BAT and CONFIG.SYS filenames to the batch file as parameters:

```
C:\> SHOWIT AUTOEXEC.BAT CONFIG.SYS
```

MS-DOS assigns the first parameter, AUTOEXEC.BAT, to the %1 variable and the second parameter, CONFIG.SYS, to the %2 variable. Within the batch file, commands can then access the parameters as shown here:

```
@ECHO OFF
TYPE %1
TYPE %2
```

MS-DOS always assigns the name of the batch file (in this case, SHOWIT) to the %0 variable. Later in this book you will learn how to use the SHIFT command to access more than nine parameters and how to test within a batch file to be sure the user has specified values for different parameters.

By using the ECHO command, you can display the values of the %0 through %9 batch-file parameters. For example, if your batch file needs to use its own name during its processing—a rare occurrence—you can use %0 to have MS-DOS provide the name.

This batch file, SHOWVAR.BAT, uses the ECHO command to display each of the %0 through %9 parameters:

```
@ECHO OFF
ECHO %0 %1 %2 %3 %4 %5 %6 %7 %8 %9
```

You can run the batch file with the following command line:

```
C:\> SHOWVAR ONE TWO THREE
```

MS-DOS then displays this:

```
C:\> SHOWVAR ONE TWO THREE
SHOWVAR ONE TWO THREE
```

Likewise, you can run the batch file with this command line:

```
C:\> SHOWVAR A B C D E F G H
```

MS-DOS then displays this:

```
C:\> SHOWVAR A B C D E F G H
SHOWVAR A B C D E F G H
```

As you can see, using batch-file parameters is essential if you want to create powerful batch files. The following batch file, CP.BAT, uses the %1 and %2 batch-file parameters to abbreviate the COPY command:

```
COPY %1 %2
```

You can run this batch file with the following command line:

```
C:\> CP \AUTOEXEC.BAT \AUTOEXEC.SAV
```

MS-DOS then assigns the parameters as follows:

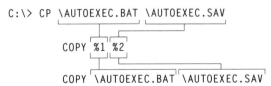

```
C:\> CP \AUTOEXEC.BAT \AUTOEXEC.SAV


         COPY %1 %2


    COPY \AUTOEXEC.BAT \AUTOEXEC.SAV
```

The previous examples have assumed that you specify a filename and extension when you invoke the batch file. The following batch file, BATEDIT.BAT, assumes you specify only a filename:

```
COPY %1.BAT %1.SAV
EDIT %1.BAT
```

In Chapter 1 you learned that you can create and edit batch files using the EDIT command provided with MS-DOS. As discussed there, when you make changes to an existing file with Edit, a copy of the original file is not saved. The BATEDIT.BAT batch file performs two tasks. First, it makes a duplicate of the batch file you are about to edit, copying the file's contents to a file with the SAV extension. Second, the batch file invokes the EDIT command so that you can make changes to the file. Assuming that you want to edit the CP.BAT batch file, you would run BATEDIT as follows:

```
C:\> BATEDIT CP
```

In this case the batch file makes the following parameter substitutions:

```
COPY %1.BAT %1.SAV ⟶ COPY CP.BAT CP.SAV
EDIT %1.BAT ⟶ EDIT CP.BAT
```

By using BATEDIT.BAT to edit your existing batch files, you can en-sure that you always have a copy of the batch file's previous contents should one of your changes cause the batch file to fail. In this case, BATEDIT.BAT provides a capability not provided with Edit. How-ever, the batch file is not perfect. If you use BATEDIT.BAT to create a new batch file, a *File not found* error message will appear briefly on your screen as the batch file executes. The error message appears because the COPY command is trying to copy a file that does not exist. In Chapter 5 you will learn how your batch files can test whether a specific file exists and then process accordingly.

Later in this book you will learn how to use the IF and FOR batch-file commands. As you will see, parameters can greatly increase the functionality of batch files that use these commands.

Batch-File Programming

TESTING SPECIFIC CONDITIONS WITHIN YOUR BATCH FILES

All the batch files we have examined so far have started with the first command in the batch file and executed the commands from top to bottom. As your batch files increase in complexity, you might want or need to control which commands MS-DOS executes, based on a specific set of conditions. The IF batch-file command gives a batch file the capability of executing an MS-DOS command only when a given condition is true.

The IF command allows a batch file to test six unique conditions: the three IF conditions—EXIST, StringOne==StringTwo, and ERROR-LEVEL—and their opposites, yielding six conditions.

Testing for an Existing File

The first IF condition tests whether a specific file exists on disk. The command format is as follows:

```
IF EXIST filename.ext DOSCommand
```

When MS-DOS encounters this form of the IF command, it examines the disk for the specified file. The filename parameter can contain a complete MS-DOS pathname—a disk-drive letter, subdirectory names, and a filename—or it can be a filename that MS-DOS will search for in the current directory. In either case, if the file exists, MS-DOS executes the specified command. If the file does not exist, MS-DOS continues with the next command in the batch file.

Testing for a Nonexisting File

Just as you can use IF EXIST to determine whether a file exists, you can use IF NOT EXIST to determine whether a file does not exist. The command format in this case is as follows:

IF NOT EXIST filename.ext DOSCommand

The effect of this form of the IF command is the opposite of the preceding form. If the file does *not* exist, MS-DOS executes the specified command. If the file does exist, MS-DOS continues with the next command in the batch file.

Putting IF EXIST to Work

To better understand the IF EXIST command, examine the batch file named T.BAT that was created in the previous chapter. This batch file displays a file using the TYPE command, as follows:

```
TYPE %1 : MORE
```

Try running this batch file, specifying a filename that does not exist in the command line. MS-DOS displays the following message:

```
File not found - filename.ext
```

The usefulness of this batch file can be greatly enhanced by including an IF EXIST command that first tests whether the specified file exists on disk. To do this, you must eliminate the redirection through MORE. If the file exists, MS-DOS executes the TYPE command. If the file does not exist, MS-DOS does not execute the TYPE command, so no error messages occur. The new T.BAT file looks like this:

```
IF EXIST %1 TYPE %1
```

Experiment with this batch file by running it with existing files as well as with files that do not exist.

In Chapter 4, you created the BATEDIT.BAT batch file, which used the following commands to copy the contents of a specified batch file to a file with the SAV extension and then loaded the batch file into Edit:

```
COPY %1.BAT %1.SAV
EDIT %1.BAT
```

As briefly discussed, if the specified batch file does not exist, the COPY command displays a *File not found* error message. Using the IF

EXIST command, however, you can change the batch file as follows to perform the COPY operation only if the specified batch file exists:

```
@ECHO OFF
IF EXIST %1.BAT COPY %1.BAT %1.SAV
EDIT %1.BAT
```

As you know, in MS-DOS versions 6.0 and earlier, the COPY command overwrites an existing file on disk if the file is not a read-only, system, or hidden file. To prevent an errant COPY command from overwriting a critical file, you might want to create a simple batch file named MYCOPY.BAT that uses the IF EXIST batch-file command to determine whether the target file already exists on disk. If the target file exists, the batch file can use the PAUSE batch-file command to warn you. You can then press any key to continue the file copy operation. Alternatively, you can press Ctrl-C to terminate the batch file.

IF EXIST Batch-File Command

Function:

Tests whether a file exists and, if it does, executes the specified MS-DOS command.

Format:

IF EXIST filename.ext DOSCommand

Notes:

The IF EXIST condition searches the disk for the specified file. The filename can be a complete MS-DOS pathname or the name of a file located in the current directory.

If MS-DOS locates the specified file, MS-DOS executes the specified command. If the file does not exist, MS-DOS continues batch-file execution with the next command in the batch file.

Example:

The following batch file tests whether the AUTOEXEC.BAT file exists in the root directory. If the file exists, the batch file displays a copy of it and then proceeds to the VER command. If the file does not exist, MS-DOS continues batch-file execution with the VER command:

```
IF EXIST \AUTOEXEC.BAT TYPE \AUTOEXEC.BAT
VER
```

For example, if you run a batch file named MYCOPY.BAT that contains these commands:

```
@ECHO OFF
IF EXIST %2 ECHO Target file already exists
ECHO Press Ctrl-C to cancel the copy
PAUSE
COPY %1 %2
```

and if the specified file exists on disk, the batch file displays this:

```
Target file already exists
Press Ctrl-C to cancel the copy
Press any key to continue . . .
```

NOTE: *Even if the user continues, the result of the file copy operation will be the message* Access denied - filename.ext *if the target file's read-only, system, or hidden attribute is set; in none of these three cases will the target file be overwritten.*

You might even want to go one step further and include the %2 batch parameter in the message that the batch file displays, as follows:

```
@ECHO OFF
IF EXIST %2 ECHO Target file %2 already exists
ECHO Press Ctrl-C to cancel the copy
PAUSE
COPY %1 %2
```

In this case, if you run the batch file with AUTOEXEC.BAT as the specified file, the batch file displays:

```
Target file AUTOEXEC.BAT already exists
Press Ctrl-C to cancel the copy
Press any key to continue . . .
```

You now know immediately why the batch file is displaying the message.

Testing for Equal Character Strings

The third IF condition tests whether two character strings are equal. A character string is a sequence of one or more characters. The format of this IF condition is as follows:

    IF StringOne==StringTwo DOSCommand

If the character strings on both sides of the double equal sign are the same, MS-DOS executes the specified command. If the strings differ, MS-DOS continues execution with the next command in the batch file.

IF StringOne==StringTwo Batch-File Command

Function:

Tests whether two character strings are identical and, if so, executes the specified MS-DOS command.

Format:

IF StringOne==StringTwo DOSCommand

Notes:

The IF StringOne==StringTwo condition compares two character strings letter by letter. If the strings match exactly, including use of uppercase and lowercase, MS-DOS executes the command that follows. If one or more letters differ, MS-DOS continues batch-file processing with the next command in the batch file.

If you do not specify two character strings in the IF command line, MS-DOS displays the error message *Syntax error*. This error is common when you are testing a batch-file parameter that does not have a value, such as this:

```
IF %1==MONTHLY_BACKUP ECHO MONTHLY
```

If you do not specify a value for %1, the IF condition becomes this:

```
IF ==MONTHLY_BACKUP ECHO MONTHLY
```

Because the command contains only one string, MS-DOS displays the *Syntax error* message. To avoid the error message, simply place the character strings to be compared within quotes, as follows:

```
IF "%1"=="MONTHLY_BACKUP" ECHO MONTHLY
```

Then, if you don't specify a value for %1, MS-DOS compares the empty string with the MONTHLY_BACKUP string, as follows:

```
IF ""=="MONTHLY_BACKUP" ECHO MONTHLY
```

Because the command line now contains two strings, MS-DOS does not generate the *Syntax error* message.

Example:

The following batch file tests whether the value of the command-line parameter is \AUTOEXEC.BAT. If it is, the batch file displays the contents of the AUTOEXEC.BAT file:

```
IF "%1"=="\AUTOEXEC.BAT" TYPE \AUTOEXEC.BAT
```

The strings are compared for an exact match including uppercase versus lowercase.

The primary use of this form of the IF command is to test the value assigned to a batch parameter. For example, the following batch file, IF-TEST.BAT, tests whether the value of the first parameter (%1) is AUTOEXEC.BAT:

```
@ECHO OFF
IF %1==AUTOEXEC.BAT ECHO Parameter is AUTOEXEC.BAT
```

Run the batch file as follows:

```
C:\> IFTEST AUTOEXEC.BAT
```

Because the parameter is equal to the characters *AUTOEXEC.BAT*, the batch file displays the following message:

```
Parameter is AUTOEXEC.BAT
```

As the complexity of your batch files increases, you will use this form of the IF command regularly.

Testing for Unequal Character Strings

Just as MS-DOS lets you test whether two strings are the same, you can use IF to determine whether two strings are different. The fourth IF condition uses the NOT operator to determine whether two character strings are *not* equal. The format is as follows:

IF NOT StringOne==StringTwo DOSCommand

If the two strings differ, MS-DOS executes the specified command. If the two strings are the same, MS-DOS continues execution with the next batch-file command.

Either of the two strings can be supplied by command-line parameters. For example, the following batch file, IFTEST2.BAT, displays a message if the command-line parameter does not equal AUTOEXEC.BAT:

```
@ECHO OFF
IF %1==AUTOEXEC.BAT ECHO Parameter is AUTOEXEC.BAT
IF NOT %1==AUTOEXEC.BAT ECHO Parameter is not AUTOEXEC.BAT
```

Putting String Tests to Work

In Chapter 8, you will learn how to use the ANSI.SYS device driver to set your screen colors. For now, you can use the IF command in a batch file to determine the color specified on the batch file's command line.

The following batch file, COLOR.BAT, examines the color name specified as the first command-line parameter:

```
@ECHO OFF
IF %1==RED ECHO Color is Red
IF %1==BLUE ECHO Color is Blue
IF %1==WHITE ECHO Color is White
```

For example, you can run the COLOR.BAT batch file with the following command line:

```
C:\> COLOR BLUE
```

The batch file then displays this:

```
Color is Blue
```

You can also run this batch file with the command line:

```
C:\> COLOR RED
```

MS-DOS then matches the expression as follows:

```
IF %1==RED ECHO Color is Red
```

The batch file then displays this:

```
Color is Red
```

For the IF command to consider two strings equal, the strings must match letter for letter, including use of uppercase and lowercase. For example, you can run the batch file with the following command line:

```
C:\> COLOR Blue
```

MS-DOS does not find a matching color because the IF command considers the strings *Blue* and *BLUE* to be different.

To better understand the way MS-DOS processes the IF command, remove the ECHO OFF command from the preceding batch file. If you then run the batch file with the following command line, you can see the actual comparisons MS-DOS performs.

```
C:\> COLOR BLUE
```

Next try running the batch file without a command-line parameter:

```
C:\> COLOR
```

Each time MS-DOS attempts to execute an IF command, it displays the message shown on the following page because the format, or syntax, of the IF command is invalid.

```
Syntax error
```

Remember: This form of the IF command compares two strings. If you do not assign a value to the %1 parameter, the IF command has only one string to compare. The parameter does not exist. Because MS-DOS requires two strings, MS-DOS displays a syntax-error message.

To prevent this problem, you need to ensure that the IF command always has two strings to compare, by enclosing the strings in double quotation marks. This results in an entry of "" if %1 does not exist. The batch file now looks like this:

```
IF "%1"=="RED" ECHO Color is Red
IF "%1"=="BLUE" ECHO Color is Blue
IF "%1"=="WHITE" ECHO Color is White
```

Then you can run the batch file with this command line:

```
C:\> COLOR BLUE
```

MS-DOS matches the condition:

```
"BLUE"=="BLUE"
```

If you run the batch file without entering a parameter, the comparison becomes this:

```
IF ""=="RED" ECHO Color is Red
```

The double quotation marks enclosing nothing are called an *empty string*. Because the IF command can compare the empty string with the color values, you have eliminated the syntax error.

In many batch files, you will need to test whether a value for %1 has been specified on the command line. The following batch file, TEST%1.BAT, uses the empty string to do just that:

```
IF "%1"=="" ECHO No parameter value specified
```

You can run the batch file with the following command line:

```
C:\> TEST%1
```

The expression then becomes this:

```
IF ""=="" ECHO No parameter value specified
```

MS-DOS displays the following message:

```
No parameter value specified
```

Testing for an Equal or Greater Exit-Status Value

Many MS-DOS commands and programs provide exit-status values to
indicate whether they were successfully executed, and if they weren't,
the cause of the error. For example, the DISKCOPY command returns
one of the following exit-status values:

Value	Meaning
0	Successful disk copy
1	Copy unsuccessful due to nonfatal disk error
2	Copy incomplete because the user pressed Ctrl-C
3	Copy unsuccessful due to fatal disk error
4	Insufficient memory or invalid drive

The IF ERRORLEVEL command lets your batch files examine another
command's exit-status value and continue processing accordingly. The
format of the IF ERRORLEVEL command is as follows:

    IF ERRORLEVEL value DOSCommand

When MS-DOS encounters an IF ERRORLEVEL command, it examines the exit-status value of the preceding command. If the exit status
value is greater than or equal to the specified value, MS-DOS executes
the specified command. If the exit-status value is less than the specified
value, MS-DOS continues processing with the next command in the
batch file.

For example, the following batch command displays an error message
if a program called SOMEPROG.EXE ends with an exit status greater
than or equal to 1:

```
SOMEPROG
IF ERRORLEVEL 1 ECHO Program experienced an error!
```

Putting IF ERRORLEVEL to Work

If the DISKCOPY command is terminated with the Ctrl-C key combination, DISKCOPY returns an exit-status value of 2. The following batch
file, ERRLEVEL.BAT, tests whether the command has been terminated:

```
@DISKCOPY A: B:
@IF ERRORLEVEL 2 ECHO Ctrl-C Termination
```

You run ERRLEVEL.BAT with the following command line:

```
C:\> ERRLEVEL
```

DISKCOPY then displays this prompt:

```
Insert SOURCE diskette in drive A:

Insert TARGET diskette in drive B:

Press any key to continue . . .
```

IF ERRORLEVEL Batch-File Command

Function:

Tests the exit-status value of the previous program. If the program's exit-status value is greater than or equal to the specified value, executes the specified MS-DOS command.

Format:

IF ERRORLEVEL value DOSCommand

Notes:

Many programs and MS-DOS commands return an exit-status value that indicates whether they successfully completed execution. For example, the FORMAT command returns the following exit-status values:

Value	Meaning
0	Successful format
3	Format incomplete because the user pressed Ctrl-C
4	Format incomplete due to an error
5	Format terminated in response to the prompt

Not all MS-DOS commands provide exit-status values.

The IF ERRORLEVEL command lets your batch files test a program's exit-status value and then continue processing accordingly. When MS-DOS encounters an IF ERRORLEVEL command, it compares the exit-status value of the preceding MS-DOS command with the value specfied in the IF command. If the exit-status value is greater than or equal to the value specified by the IF command, MS-DOS executes the corresponding command. If the exit-status value is less than the specified value, MS-DOS continues with the next command in the batch file. (This logic is reversed if the IF NOT ERRORLEVEL command is used.)

If you press Ctrl-C to terminate the command, MS-DOS displays this:

```
Ctrl-C Termination
```

When you terminate the DISKCOPY command, MS-DOS continues the batch file's execution with the IF command, comparing DISKCOPY's

---

Example:

The following batch file executes the FORMAT command and displays a completion-status message based on FORMAT's exit-status value:

```
@ECHO OFF
FORMAT A:
IF ERRORLEVEL 5 GOTO NO_RESPONSE
IF ERRORLEVEL 4 GOTO ERROR
IF ERRORLEVEL 3 GOTO USER_CTRLC
ECHO Successful FORMAT operation
GOTO DONE
:NO_RESPONSE
ECHO Fixed disk will not be formatted
GOTO DONE
:ERROR
ECHO Error in processing, FORMAT incomplete
GOTO DONE
:USER_CTRLC
ECHO FORMAT incomplete due to Ctrl-C
:DONE
```

Notice that the batch file tests the highest exit-status value first.

Remember: If the exit-status value is greater than or equal to the value specified by the IF command, MS-DOS executes the specified command. If this batch file first tested for an exit-status value of 3, MS-DOS would always perform the processing that follows the :USERCTRLC label, whether the exit-status value was 3, 4, or 5, because the exit-status value would always be greater than or equal to 3. By reversing the order of the tests, the batch file branches to the correct set of commands for each exit-status value.

You can test for a specific exit-status value by combining IF ERROR-LEVEL with IF NOT ERRORLEVEL. For example, you could test for an exit-status value of 3 with this command:

```
IF ERRORLEVEL 3 IF NOT ERRORLEVEL 4 GOTO USER_CTRLC
```

exit-status value with the value 2. Because the values are equal, MS-DOS displays this message:

```
Ctrl-C Termination
```

NOTE: *As long as the preceding command's exit-status value is greater than or equal to the specified value, MS-DOS executes the command specified by the IF command. If DISKCOPY terminates because of fatal disk error or insufficient memory or invalid drive (exit-status values 3 and 4, respectively), the condition tested by the IF command would also be true, and the specified MS-DOS command would be executed.*

Testing for an Exit-Status Value Less Than a Specific Value

Using the NOT operator with the IF ERRORLEVEL command, your batch files can test whether an exit-status value is less than a specific value. If the exit-status value is less than the specified value, MS-DOS executes the specified command; otherwise, it continues processing with the next command in the batch file. The format of the IF NOT ERRORLEVEL command is as follows:

IF NOT ERRORLEVEL value DOSCommand

Testing for Specific ERRORLEVEL Values

As your batch files become more complex, you might need to combine an IF ERRORLEVEL command with an IF NOT ERRORLEVEL command to test for specific exit-status values. For example, the following batch commands test for exit-status values from 0 through 4 following a DISKCOPY command:

```
@ECHO OFF
DISKCOPY A: B:
IF ERRORLEVEL 0 IF NOT ERRORLEVEL 1 ECHO Exit status 0
IF ERRORLEVEL 1 IF NOT ERRORLEVEL 2 ECHO Exit status 1
IF ERRORLEVEL 2 IF NOT ERRORLEVEL 3 ECHO Exit status 2
IF ERRORLEVEL 3 IF NOT ERRORLEVEL 4 ECHO Exit status 3
IF ERRORLEVEL 4 IF NOT ERRORLEVEL 5 ECHO Exit status 4
```

In the first IF command, the first test (IF ERRORLEVEL 0) ensures that the exit-status value is at least 0. The second test (IF NOT ERRORLEVEL 1) ensures that the exit-status value is less than 1. By combining these two tests, the command ensures that the exit-status value is 0. Likewise, the second IF command ensures that the exit-status value is 1, and so on.

The capability of testing and using exit-status values is the key to increasing the functionality of the batch files that appear later in this book. Your goal in creating a batch file is to automate a series of MS-DOS commands. With that in mind, your batch files should be able to handle unexpected errors. The IF ERRORLEVEL command lets your batch files do exactly that. Later in this section, you will use the CHOICE command, introduced with MS-DOS version 6, to evaluate different exit-status values that result depending on the keyboard response of the batch-file user.

UNDERSTANDING THE *NOT* OPERATOR

As you just learned, the IF command lets your batch files execute an MS-DOS command only if a specific condition is met. The condition can be the existence of a particular file, two strings being identical, or a command's exit-status value being greater than or equal to a specified value. You've also seen that the opposite of these conditions (a file doesn't exist, two strings are not equal, or an exit-status value is less than a specified value) are tested with the NOT operator.

The NOT operator changes the result of a condition. For example, if a condition is true, using the NOT operator makes it false. On the other hand, if the condition is false, using the NOT operator makes it true.

You can make your batch files perform different actions based on the results of a single condition by using two IF statements, one of which uses NOT. Earlier in this chapter you created the T.BAT batch file, which tests whether the file specified by %1 exists on disk and, if it does, displays the file's contents. You can modify the batch file to perform a second test that allows the batch file to display this message:

filename.ext does not exist

The modified T.BAT batch file looks like this:

```
@ECHO OFF
IF EXIST %1 TYPE %1
IF NOT EXIST %1 ECHO %1 does not exist
```

Now if the result of the EXIST %1 condition is false (meaning the file does not exist), the NOT operator changes the result to true, and

NOT Batch-File Operator

Function:

Reverses a true or false result in an IF command. If the result of a test is false, NOT changes the result to true. Conversely, if the result of a test is true, NOT changes the result to false.

Format:

IF NOT condition DOSCommand

Notes:

The NOT operator can be used with any of the three IF conditions:

```
IF NOT EXIST filename.ext DOSCommand
IF NOT StringOne==StringTwo DOSCommand
IF NOT ERRORLEVEL value DOSCommand
```

Example:

The following batch file tests whether the AUTOEXEC.BAT file is in the root directory of the current drive. If it isn't, the batch file displays messages that tell you to create the file.

```
@ECHO OFF
IF NOT EXIST \AUTOEXEC.BAT GOTO NO_FILE
GOTO DONE
:NO_FILE
ECHO Your root directory does not contain the batch
ECHO file AUTOEXEC.BAT. This batch file lets you
ECHO specify one or more commands that you want MS-DOS
ECHO to execute each time your system starts. Most
ECHO users place the MS-DOS PRINT, PROMPT, and PATH
ECHO commands in this file.
:DONE
```

If the AUTOEXEC.BAT file does not reside in the root directory of the default drive, the batch file displays this:

```
Your root directory does not contain the batch
file AUTOEXEC.BAT. This batch file lets you
specify one or more commands that you want MS-DOS
to execute each time your system starts. Most
users place the MS-DOS PRINT, PROMPT, and PATH
commands in this file.
```

MS-DOS executes the ECHO command. If the result of the EXIST %1 condition is true (meaning the file exists), the NOT operator changes the result to false, and MS-DOS does not execute the ECHO command.

The NOT operator is used extensively in MS-DOS batch files. Here's another example. The following batch file, COMPSTR.BAT, compares the two strings contained in the batch parameters %1 and %2. If the strings are identical, the batch file displays this message:

string1 and *string2* are identical

If the strings are different, the batch file displays this message:

string1 and *string2* are not the same

This batch file's commands are as follows:

```
@ECHO OFF
IF "%1"=="%2" ECHO %1 and %2 are identical
IF NOT "%1"=="%2" ECHO %1 and %2 are not the same
```

As you can see, the batch file needs two IF commands to perform its processing. The first IF command handles the condition where the strings are the same. The second IF command handles the condition where the strings are different. (Programmers will recognize the similarity to an IF-THEN-ELSE statement.)

BRANCHING WITH GOTO

All the batch files we have examined so far have started with the first command in the batch file and executed commands one after another from top to bottom. When we discussed the IF command, you saw that you can direct MS-DOS to execute a command only when a specific condition is met. As your applications increase in complexity, you might occasionally need to direct MS-DOS to perform a specific set of commands under certain circumstances or to skip one or more commands under others. The GOTO command lets your batch file direct, or *branch*, processing control from one command to another. The format of the GOTO batch command is as follows:

GOTO DOSBatchLabel

Now let's take a look at a simple example. The following batch file, REMOVE.BAT, uses the %1 parameter to display a file's contents and then, unless you stop the batch file with Ctrl-C, deletes the file:

```
@ECHO OFF
IF "%1"=="" GOTO NO_FILE
TYPE %1
ECHO About to delete %1
ECHO Press Ctrl-C to stop
PAUSE
DEL %1
GOTO DONE
:NO_FILE
ECHO Need to specify filename
:DONE
```

When you run the batch file, REMOVE.BAT begins by testing whether you specified a file as a command-line parameter. If you didn't, the batch file branches to the label NO_FILE, as follows:

```
@ECHO OFF
IF "%1"=="" GOTO NO_FILE ──┐
TYPE %1                    │
ECHO About to delete %1    │
ECHO Press Ctrl-C to stop  │
PAUSE                      │
DEL %1                     │
GOTO DONE                  │
:NO_FILE ◄─────────────────┘
ECHO Need to specify filename
:DONE
```

The batch file displays the following message and then ends:

```
Need to specify filename
```

If you specified a file, the batch file displays the file's contents and then displays this message:

```
About to delete filename.ext
Press Ctrl-C to stop
Press any key to continue . . .
```

If you press a key to delete the file, the batch file issues the DEL command and then uses GOTO to branch to the :DONE label at the end of the batch file. If you don't want to delete the file, you can terminate the batch file by pressing Ctrl-C.

As you can see, the GOTO command branches to the specified label. A batch label must begin with a colon and can contain any number of characters—although MS-DOS recognizes only the first eight. This batch file uses the labels :NO_FILE and :DONE. Notice that the line containing the label begins with a colon and that the label reference in the GOTO command does not:

```
@ECHO OFF
IF "%1"=="" GOTO NO_FILE ─────────────┬───────── Label references in
TYPE %1                                           GOTO commands
ECHO About to delete %1
ECHO Press Ctrl-C to stop
PAUSE
DEL %1
GOTO DONE ────────────────────────────┘
:NO_FILE ─────────────────────────────┐
ECHO Need to specify filename         ├───────── MS-DOS labels with colons
:DONE ────────────────────────────────┘
```

When MS-DOS encounters a line in your batch file that begins with a colon, MS-DOS knows that the line contains a label and does not attempt to execute the label as a command. Regardless of the state of ECHO, MS-DOS does not display labels when executing a batch file.

Applications for batch files are basically limitless. For example, the next batch file we'll look at, ADDRBOOK.BAT, provides an online address book that contains important addresses and phone numbers. To use the batch file, you specify a person's name (in uppercase letters), and the batch file displays the person's phone number and address as shown here:

```
C:\> ADDRBOOK SMITH
Gary Smith
28000 South 5th Street
Seattle, Washington 98444
(206) 555-5555
```

If you specify the name of a person who is not included in the address book, the batch file displays this message:

```
C:> ADDRBOOK KAHN
No such entry KAHN
```

The following batch file implements ADDRBOOK.BAT:

```
@ECHO OFF
IF "%1"=="" GOTO NO NAME
IF "%1"=="SMITH" GOTO SMITH
IF "%1"=="JONES" GOTO JONES
IF "%1"=="ALLEN" GOTO ALLEN
ECHO No such entry %1
GOTO DONE
```

(continued)

GOTO Batch-File Command

Function:

Directs, or *branches*, processing from one command in a batch file to another location identified with a label.

Format:

GOTO DOSBatchLabel

The location to branch to is identified with the following:

:DOSBatchLabel

Notes:

By default, MS-DOS processes the statements in a batch file starting with the first command and executing each command in order from the top to bottom. The GOTO command causes MS-DOS to jump to a new location within the batch file (identified with a label) and to continue executing with the command following the label. This branching capability enables you to create batch files that repeat commands and that perform different actions based upon a condition.

A label is identified by placing a colon (:) before the label name. Only the first eight characters of the label name are used to identify the label. As a result, the labels :BATCHFILE1 and :BATCHFILE2 are the same. In the GOTO command, the label is referenced without the colon.

The GOTO command is most often used with the IF command to perform different tasks within the batch file based on the condition tested by the IF statement. The GOTO and IF ERRORLEVEL commands can be used with the CHOICE command to select a task based upon the key pressed by the user. (See the discussion of the CHOICE command.) By itself, GOTO is used to create loops and to branch back to the main portion of the batch file after performing a task set by an IF statement.

Examples:

The following batch file uses the IF condition to test the value specified on the command line. This value represents the language that is used to determine which section of the batch file is processed.

```
@ECHO OFF
IF"%1"=="GERMAN" GOTO GERMAN
IF"%1"=="FRENCH" GOTO FRENCH
IF"%1"=="SWEDISH" GOTO SWEDISH
GOTO INVALID_LANGUAGE
```

```
:GERMAN
ECHO You picked German.
GOTO DONE
:FRENCH
ECHO You picked French.
GOTO DONE
:SWEDISH
Echo You picked Swedish.
GOTO DONE
:INVALID_LANGUAGE
ECHO That language is not available.
:DONE
```

The batch file compares the value of %1 with the acceptable options (GERMAN, FRENCH, or SWEDISH). If %1 matches one of these options, the batch file branches to the corresponding label. If %1 does not match any of the options, the batch file branches to the INVALID_-LANGUAGE label. (MS-DOS recognizes the label as INVALID_, so avoid using more than one label starting with INVALID_.) After the tasks are performed for the selected language, another GOTO branches to the end of the file (skipping the sections for the other languages).

The next batch file repeatedly displays a menu and uses the CHOICE command to obtain a response from the user:

```
@ECHO OFF
:LOOP
ECHO Press N for a directory listing sorted by Name.
ECHO Press E for a directory listing sorted by Extension.
ECHO Press Q to Quit.
CHOICE /N /CNEQ Select an option:
IF ERRORLEVEL 1 IF NOT ERRORLEVEL 2 DIR /ON
IF ERRORLEVEL 2 IF NOT ERRORLEVEL 3 DIR /OE
IF ERRORLEVEL 3 GOTO DONE
GOTO LOOP
:DONE
```

The first set of ECHO commands displays the menu choices. The CHOICE command is used to obtain a response from the user that is stored as the ERRORLEVEL (we explain this further in the discussion of the CHOICE command). Based on the value of ERRORLEVEL, one of the tasks is performed. Unless the user chooses to exit the menu, GOTO LOOP causes the menu to be displayed again, and CHOICE waits for another response. This process continues until the Q option is selected (or the user stops the batch file with Ctrl-C).

```
:SMITH
ECHO Gary Smith
ECHO 28000 South 5th Street
ECHO Seattle, Washington 98444
ECHO (206) 555-5555
GOTO DONE

:JONES
ECHO Alex Jones
ECHO 12345 Second Street
ECHO Phoenix, Arizona 85023
ECHO (602) 555-5555
GOTO DONE

:ALLEN
ECHO Joe Allen
ECHO 1321 Main Street
ECHO Las Vegas, Nevada 89119
ECHO (702) 555-5555
GOTO DONE

:NO_NAME
ECHO No name specified
:DONE
```

As you can see, the batch file simply examines the contents of the first parameter and determines which phone number and address you want. Because the IF command considers upper- and lowercase letters to be different, you must specify the name in uppercase.

If your computer has a modem, you can create a batch file named AUTOCALL.BAT that automatically dials the phone number you want. Assuming that your modem is connected to COM1, the batch file looks like this:

```
@ECHO OFF
IF "%1"=="" GOTO NO_NAME
IF "%1"=="SMITH" ECHO ATDT 1-206-555-5555 > COM1
IF "%1"=="JONES" ECHO ATDT 1-602-555-5555 > COM1
IF "%1"=="ALLEN" ECHO ATDT 1-702-555-5555 > COM1
PAUSE
ECHO ATH > COM1
:NO_NAME
```

In this case, the batch file uses ECHO to output the modem commands necessary to dial the phone. When the phone rings, you can pick it up and have your conversation. When you are done, you can press any key in response to the batch file's PAUSE command, and the batch file will issue the commands necessary to hang up the phone.

GETTING USER CHOICES

Beginning with MS-DOS version 6, you can use the CHOICE command in your batch files to prompt for and evaluate a keyboard response. By default, the CHOICE command displays a prompt and evaluates whether the response to a question is *Y* for Yes or *N* for No. For example, if your batch file needs to know whether to print the contents of the CONFIG.SYS file, you can use the following CHOICE command:

```
CHOICE Do you want to print CONFIG.SYS
```

This displays the following message:

```
Do you want to print CONFIG.SYS[Y,N]?
```

If the user presses anything other than Y or N, CHOICE sounds a beep on your computer's built-in speaker and continues to wait for a correct response. In this case, pressing Y returns the exit-status value 1, and pressing N returns the value 2. Within your batch file, you can include the following IF ERRORLEVEL command to print the file if the response is Y:

```
IF ERRORLEVEL 1 IF NOT ERRORLEVEL 2 PRINT \CONFIG.SYS
```

If you want the user to choose from a different set of keys, use the /C option of the CHOICE command, which enables you to specify the set of keys. For example, the following CHOICE command gives the user the choice of pressing the 1, 2, 3, or 4 key:

```
CHOICE /C:1234 Select an option:
```

The set of keys that follow CHOICE's /C switch specify the keystrokes for which CHOICE will wait. If any other key is pressed, CHOICE sounds a beep and continues to wait for a specified keystroke. When a specified key is pressed, CHOICE returns an exit-status value that corresponds to the chosen key's position in the set following the /C switch. In this case, CHOICE displays the prompt *Select an option:[1,2,3,4]?* and then returns an exit-status value of 1 if you press 1, 2 if you press 2, 3 for 3, and 4 for 4. Likewise, the following command displays the prompt *Select an option:[A,B,C,D]?* and then returns an exit-status value of 1 if you press A, 2 if you press B, 3 for C, and 4 for D:

```
CHOICE /C:ABCD Select an option:
```

If you press the Ctrl-C keyboard combination to cancel the CHOICE command, CHOICE returns an exit-status value of 0.

You can then use the IF ERRORLEVEL command to determine which key was pressed. For example, the next batch file, 1_CHOICE.BAT, prompts you to press the A, B, C, or D key and then displays on the screen which key was pressed:

```
@ECHO OFF
CHOICE /C:ABCD Press one of the following keys:
IF ERRORLEVEL 0 IF NOT ERRORLEVEL 1 ECHO Ctrl-C
IF ERRORLEVEL 1 IF NOT ERRORLEVEL 2 ECHO You pressed A
IF ERRORLEVEL 2 IF NOT ERRORLEVEL 3 ECHO You pressed B
IF ERRORLEVEL 3 IF NOT ERRORLEVEL 4 ECHO You pressed C
IF ERRORLEVEL 4 IF NOT ERRORLEVEL 5 ECHO You pressed D
```

NOTE: *You will see only the* Ctrl-C *message if you press* N *in response to the* Terminate batch job (y/n)? *prompt.*

One of the most common uses of the CHOICE command is to process a menu of options. The following batch file, MENU_CH.BAT, displays such a menu, determines which key was pressed, and runs the program specified by the user's choice:

```
@ECHO OFF
:LOOP
CLS
ECHO        Main Menu
ECHO.
ECHO   A    Run MSAV (Virus Protection)
ECHO   B    Run DEFRAG (Disk Defragmentation)
ECHO   C    Run MEM (Memory Use Display)
ECHO   Q    Quit to DOS
ECHO.
CHOICE /C:ABCQ Enter choice:
IF NOT ERRORLEVEL 1 GOTO DONE
IF ERRORLEVEL 1 IF NOT ERRORLEVEL 2 MSAV
IF ERRORLEVEL 2 IF NOT ERRORLEVEL 3 DEFRAG
IF ERRORLEVEL 3 IF NOT ERRORLEVEL 4 MEM /DEBUG /PAGE
IF ERRORLEVEL 4 GOTO DONE
PAUSE
GOTO LOOP
:DONE
```

You could use similar commands to modify your AUTOEXEC.BAT file to display a menu of command options each time your system starts.

Suppressing the Display of Valid Keys

By default, CHOICE displays in its prompt the keys that can be pressed. For example, you can insert the following CHOICE command in a batch file:

```
CHOICE /C:ABCD Select an option:
```

You see this prompt when the CHOICE command is executed:

```
Select an option:[A,B,C,D]?
```

In some cases, you may not want CHOICE to display a list of valid keys. For example, displaying all the valid keys for a menu that has several options could be distracting. You can direct CHOICE not to display the keys by including the /N switch in CHOICE's command line. For example, the following CHOICE command includes the /N switch:

```
CHOICE /C:ABCD /N Select an option:
```

When MS-DOS executes this command, CHOICE displays this prompt:

```
Select an option:
```

As you can see, CHOICE suppresses not only the display of valid keys but also the question mark (?) that appears after the valid keys.

Specifying a Default CHOICE Option

Many people include the CHOICE command in their AUTO-EXEC.BAT files in order to control the commands MS-DOS executes each time the system starts. For example, if you don't want MS-DOS to run the MSAV virus-detection utility every time you turn on your computer, you can include the following commands in your AUTO-EXEC.BAT file:

```
CHOICE Do you want to execute MSAV
IF ERRORLEVEL 1 IF NOT ERRORLEVEL 2 MSAV
```

By using CHOICE in this way, you have complete control over your system startup. Unfortunately, using these commands also means that you must be at your keyboard when your system starts in order to respond to each prompt. Otherwise, MS-DOS will simply sit at the first CHOICE command, waiting for your response.

To prevent your system from stopping in this way, you can specify a default option that CHOICE can select if no response is given in a specified number of seconds. For example, suppose you want CHOICE to assume your answer is N if you don't respond to the prompt within 15 seconds. You can include in your batch file a CHOICE command that includes the /T switch, as follows:

```
CHOICE /T:N,15 Do you want to execute MSAV
IF ERRORLEVEL 1 IF NOT ERRORLEVEL 2 MSAV
```

CHOICE's /T switch lets you select a default option and the number of seconds (from 0 to 99) after which MS-DOS should select that option. In our example, after 15 seconds the CHOICE command behaves as if you have pressed the N key, returning the exit-status value 2.

Treating Uppercase and Lowercase Choices Differently

Unless you specify otherwise, CHOICE considers uppercase and lowercase letters to be the same. For example, the following CHOICE command waits for the user to type *A*, *B*, *C*, or *D*:

CHOICE Batch-File Command

Function:

Displays a message and then waits for the user to press one of a predefined set of keys. CHOICE then returns an exit-status value from which the batch file can determine the key pressed.

Format:

CHOICE [/C[:]Keys] [/N] [/S] [/T[:]Default,Seconds][Prompt]

Notes:

When a batch file executes a CHOICE command, CHOICE waits for the user to press one of a specified set of keys. If the user presses a key not specified in the set, CHOICE causes the computer's built-in speaker to sound a beep and waits until a correct key is pressed. When the user presses a correct key, CHOICE returns an exit-status value that the batch file can test using IF ERRORLEVEL to determine which key was pressed. The exit-status value returned depends on the key pressed and the order of the keys following the CHOICE command's /C switch. CHOICE returns an exit-status value of 1 for the first key, 2 for the second, and so on.

The /C switch specifies the set of keys the user can press. If you don't include the /C switch, CHOICE assumes you are prompting the user for a Y (yes) or N (no) response.

By default, CHOICE displays the set of valid keys and a question mark immediately following the user prompt. If you include the /N switch, CHOICE displays neither the keys nor the question mark.

```
CHOICE /C:ABCD Select an option:
```

In this case, CHOICE returns the same exit-status value whether you type *A* or *a*.

For those times when you want CHOICE to treat uppercase and lowercase letters differently, you can include the /S switch to tell CHOICE to distinguish between uppercase and lowercase letters. For example, the following batch file, SORTMENU.BAT, displays a menu that lets you display a directory listing sorted in six ways. As you can see, the six options correspond to the letters N, n, E, e, S, and s:

Also by default, CHOICE considers uppercase and lowercase letters to be the same. If you include the /S switch, CHOICE distinguishes between uppercase and lowercase letters.

The /T switch lets you specify a default key and the number of seconds (from 0 through 99) after which CHOICE automatically selects the default.

NOTE: *CHOICE is an external MS-DOS command and must be either in the current directory or on the search path.*

Examples:

The following CHOICE command prompts the user to indicate whether MS-DOS should print the AUTOEXEC.BAT file:

```
CHOICE Do you want to print AUTOEXEC.BAT
```

In this case, because the CHOICE command line does not include a /C switch, CHOICE prompts for a Y or N response.

The next CHOICE command displays the prompt *Select an option:* and then waits for the user to press the A, B, C, or Q key.

```
CHOICE /C:ABCQ Select an option:
```

The last command example prompts the user to indicate whether MS-DOS should execute the MSAV anti-virus utility. If the user does not respond within 15 seconds, CHOICE selects N as the default response:

```
CHOICE /T:N,15 Do you want to run MSAV
```

```
@ECHO OFF
CLS
ECHO        Sort Menu
ECHO.
ECHO   N    Sort files by name A-Z
ECHO   n    Sort files by name Z-A
ECHO   E    Sort files by extension A-Z
ECHO   e    Sort files by extension Z-A
ECHO   S    Sort files by size smallest-largest
ECHO   s    Sort files by size largest-smallest
ECHO.
CHOICE /C:NnEeSs /S /N Sort Option:
IF NOT ERRORLEVEL 1 GOTO DONE
IF ERRORLEVEL 1 IF NOT ERRORLEVEL 2 DIR /O:N
IF ERRORLEVEL 2 IF NOT ERRORLEVEL 3 DIR /O:-N
IF ERRORLEVEL 3 IF NOT ERRORLEVEL 4 DIR /O:E
IF ERRORLEVEL 4 IF NOT ERRORLEVEL 5 DIR /O:-E
IF ERRORLEVEL 5 IF NOT ERRORLEVEL 6 DIR /O:S
IF ERRORLEVEL 6 IF NOT ERRORLEVEL 7 DIR /O:-S
:DONE
```

Using CHOICE with GOTO

In many cases a user selection might result in the execution of several commands instead of only one. For example, the following batch file lets the user decide whether to perform accounts receivable, accounts payable, general ledger, or month end processing. The batch file uses the CHOICE command to obtain the user's selection and the GOTO command to branch to specific locations where several corresponding commands might be executed:

```
@ECHO OFF
:LOOP
CLS
ECHO            Accounting Main Menu
ECHO.
ECHO   A    Accounts Receivable
ECHO   B    Accounts Payable
ECHO   C    General Ledger
ECHO   D    Month End Processing
ECHO   Q    Quit
ECHO.
CHOICE /C:ABCDQ Enter choice:
IF NOT ERRORLEVEL 1 GOTO DONE
IF ERRORLEVEL 1 IF NOT ERRORLEVEL 2 GOTO ACCT_REC
IF ERRORLEVEL 2 IF NOT ERRORLEVEL 3 GOTO ACCT_PAY
IF ERRORLEVEL 3 IF NOT ERRORLEVEL 4 GOTO GENERAL_LEDGER
IF ERRORLEVEL 4 IF NOT ERRORLEVEL 5 GOTO MONTH_END
IF ERRORLEVEL 5 GOTO DONE
GOTO LOOP
```

```
:ACCT_REC
GET_RECV
PRT_RECV
ENV_RECV
GOTO LOOP

:ACCT_PAY
GET_BILL
PRT_BILL
GOTO LOOP

:GENERAL_LEDGER
GEN_LED
PRINT REPORT.GLL
GOTO LOOP

:MONTH_END
COMBINE
PRINT TOTALS.DAT
MERGE MONTH.DAT YEAR.DAT
GOTO LOOP

:DONE
```

In most cases, batch files that display a menu of options use CHOICE to get the user selection, IF ERRORLEVEL to determine the selection, and GOTO to branch to the corresponding batch-file commands.

REPEATING AN MS-DOS COMMAND FOR A SET OF FILES

As you learned earlier in this chapter, the IF command lets your batch files perform an MS-DOS command only when a specific condition exists. Processing that is dependent upon whether a specific condition is true or false is called *conditional processing*. Another batch-file command, FOR, lets your batch files repeat a command for a specific set of files. Processing that executes at least one time, possibly more, is called *iterative processing*.

Like most commands specific to batch-file processing (the exception being CHOICE), FOR is an internal command. MS-DOS always keeps internal commands in memory (unlike external commands, such as DISK-COPY, which remain on disk until they are needed).

The format of the FOR command is as follows:

FOR %%BatchVar IN (SetOfFiles) DO DOSCommand

The name of the command, FOR, is followed by the *%%BatchVar* variable. Earlier, we discussed the %0 through %9 variables to which MS-DOS assigns the values of command-line parameters during batch-file processing. MS-DOS also assigns a value to the *%%BatchVar* variable. The difference is that the meaning of the %0 through %9 variables are predefined, whereas you can choose any single letter you want, such as %%A or %%F, as your *%%BatchVar* variable. (MS-DOS restricts the names of batch-file variables to one character.)

The *%%BatchVar* variable is followed by the word IN, which tells MS-DOS that the set of values the FOR command is to use follows immediately, enclosed in parentheses. For example, you specify a set of files by simply typing filenames, separated by either a space or a comma. The following are examples of valid sets of files for the FOR command:

```
(MAY.PAY JUNE.PAY JULY.PAY)
(MAY.PAY,JUNE.PAY,JULY.PAY)
(*.BAT *.EXE *.COM)
(*.*)
```

As you can see, FOR supports the * (asterisk) wildcard character, as well as the ? (question mark). When FOR detects a wildcard, MS-DOS expands the wildcard into the corresponding set of filenames.

As the FOR command executes, MS-DOS assigns each filename in the set of files to the *%%BatchVar* variable. After the first filename is assigned, MS-DOS executes the command that follows the word *DO* in the command line. The command can be any MS-DOS command. When the command completes execution, MS-DOS assigns the second filename to the *%%BatchVar* variable, and the process repeats. When no files remain in the set, the FOR command completes execution.

To better understand this processing, consider this command:

```
FOR %%A IN (A.BAT B.BAT C.BAT) DO TYPE %%A
```

Here, FOR first assigns the A.BAT file to the %%A variable, and MS-DOS then executes the TYPE %%A command. Because MS-DOS has assigned the A.BAT filename to the *%%BatchVar* variable—%%A, in this case—MS-DOS actually executes the TYPE A.BAT command.

When the TYPE command completes execution, FOR assigns the next file in the set to the %%A variable and repeats the TYPE command. In this case, MS-DOS displays the contents of the B.BAT file. FOR repeats the process again, assigning the C.BAT file to the variable.

Finally, when the TYPE command completes execution, FOR examines the set of files and, because no more files remain, completes execution.

Showing the Directory List

In a similar manner, the next batch file, SHOW.BAT, uses the FOR command to display all the batch files in the current directory:

```
FOR %%I IN (*.BAT) DO TYPE %%I
```

This FOR command uses *%%I* as its *%%BatchVar* variable. The actual variable name does not matter as long as it is a single letter.

Here's another example. By default, the DIR command displays filenames, extensions, sizes, and creation dates and times like this:

```
TIMEDATE BAT       23 04-07-94  1:23a
DISKINFO BAT       18 04-07-94  11:13a
SHORTDIR BAT       21 04-07-94  11:15a
VERVOL2  BAT       12 04-08-94  1:23p
DIRAB    BAT       30 04-08-94  1:57p
DIRAB    OUT        0 04-08-94  1:58p
PRINTDIR BAT       41 04-09-94  2:29p
    .        .      .     .       .
    .        .      .     .       .
    .        .      .     .       .
ERRLEVEL˙BAT       73 04-15-94  5:58p
```

If you use DIR with the /W switch, MS-DOS displays only filenames and extensions in five columns across the screen. In some cases, you might want to display the filenames one after another, as follows:

```
TIMEDATE.BAT
DISKINFO.BAT
SHORTDIR.BAT
VERVOL2.BAT
DIRAB.BAT
DIRAB.OUT
PRINTDIR.BAT
    .
    .
    .
ERRLEVEL.BAT
```

The next batch file, SHORTDIR.BAT, uses the FOR command with the ECHO command to display filenames in such an arrangement on the screen:

```
@ECHO OFF
FOR %%I IN (*.*) DO ECHO %%I
```

Here, the FOR command assigns the name of each file in the current directory to the %%I variable. MS-DOS then uses the ECHO command to display the filename on the screen. (Of course, in MS-DOS versions 5 and later, you can also do this with DIR /B.)

By using batch-file parameters, you can increase the flexibility of SHORTDIR.BAT to allow you to specify the filenames you want to display as the first command-line parameter. You can then type the following to display all the files in the current directory with the BAT extension:

```
C:\> SHORTDIR *.BAT
```

To display the files with the TXT extension, you can type this:

```
C:\> SHORTDIR *.TXT
```

To display all the files in the current directory, the command line is this:

```
C:\> SHORTDIR *.*
```

To provide this flexibility, change SHORTDIR.BAT as follows:

```
@ECHO OFF
FOR %%I IN (%1) DO ECHO %%I
```

Sorting the Display

The next batch file, SORTDIR.BAT, uses the MS-DOS redirection operators with the FOR command to display a sorted directory listing of the files specified by the first command-line parameter:

```
@ECHO OFF
IF EXIST SORTFILE.DAT DEL SORTFILE.DAT
FOR %%I IN (%1) DO ECHO %%I >> SORTFILE.DAT
SORT < SORTFILE.DAT
DEL SORTFILE.DAT
```

This batch file first uses the IF EXIST command to delete the SORT-FILE.DAT file if it exists. Next the FOR command "echoes" (with ECHO) each filename (as the previous batch file did). In this case, however, the batch file uses the >> redirection operator to direct the output of the ECHO command from the screen and append the output to the SORTFILE.DAT file. After FOR has created the file of filenames, the batch file uses the SORT command to sort the file's contents, displaying the sorted filenames on the screen. When the SORT command completes execution, it deletes SORTFILE.DAT because the file is no

FOR Batch-File Command

Function:

Repeats an MS-DOS command for a given set of files.

Format:

FOR *%%BatchVar* IN (set) DO DOSCommand

Notes:

When you run the FOR command, FOR assigns the first file specified in the set of files to the specified variable. The variable's name must be a single character. You specify the set of files either by typing filenames separated by spaces or commas, or by using the * (asterisk) or ? (question mark) wildcard characters. The FOR command fully supports the MS-DOS wildcard characters. If the set of files is specified using wildcards, FOR expands each wildcard to create the appropriate set of filenames, and assigns each filename to the variable, one at a time.

After assigning a filename to the variable, FOR executes the specified MS-DOS command. When the MS-DOS command completes execution, FOR assigns the next filename in the set to the variable, and the process repeats.

When no more filenames remain in the set, the FOR command completes execution, and the batch file continues processing with the next command.

Examples:

The following batch file uses the FOR command to issue the TYPE command and display the contents of the files A.TXT, B.TXT, and C.TXT:

```
FOR %%I IN (A.TXT B.TXT C.TXT) DO TYPE %%I
```

In a similar manner, the following batch file uses the TYPE command to display the contents of all the files associated with the %1 parameter:

```
FOR %%V IN (%1) DO TYPE %%V
```

If you run the batch file with a wildcard character, such as the asterisk in *.BAT, the batch file displays the contents of each corresponding file.

longer needed. (In MS-DOS versions 5 and later, DIR /B /O:N does the same thing.)

Creating a Flexible TYPE Command

Using the FOR command, you can improve the T.BAT batch
file you created at the beginning of the chapter so that it supports the
MS-DOS wildcard characters. Make these changes:

```
@ECHO OFF
FOR %%I IN (%1) DO TYPE %%I
```

Now the following command displays the contents of all the batch files
that reside in the current directory:

```
C:\> T *.BAT
```

In fact, you might want to be able to designate specific files as FOR's
set of files by including several batch-file parameters, as follows:

```
@ECHO OFF
FOR %%I IN (%1 %2 %3 %4 %5) DO TYPE %%I
```

You can then specify which files to display with a command line such
as this:

```
C:\> T SORTDIR.BAT SHORTDIR.BAT *.BAT
```

The batch file first displays the contents of SORTDIR.BAT, followed
by those of SHORTDIR.BAT. Then the batch file displays the contents
of all the files with the BAT extension in the current drive and directory.

The FOR command adds tremendous flexibility to batch files, and we
will use it repeatedly throughout the remainder of this book.

CHAPTER 6

Advanced Batch-File Concepts

USING NAMED PARAMETERS

As you have seen, the %0 through %9 parameters increase your batch file's capabilities, allowing a single batch file to serve several purposes. In addition to these batch-file parameters, MS-DOS versions 3.3 and later support *named parameters*, which are batch-file variables enclosed in percent signs. When MS-DOS encounters a named parameter in a batch file, MS-DOS searches its environment for a corresponding entry. For example, this batch file, SHOWFILE.BAT, displays the file that corresponds to the %SHOWFILE_FILE% named parameter:

```
TYPE %SHOW_FILE% | MORE
```

When MS-DOS encounters %SHOW_FILE%, it searches its environment for an entry in the following form:

```
    SHOW_FILE=
```

The SET command allows you to change or display the entries in the MS-DOS environment. For example, you can issue the SET command without a command line, like this:

```
C:\> SET
```

MS-DOS then displays the current environment entries, as follows:

```
COMSPEC=C:\DOS\COMMAND.COM
PATH=C:\DOS
PROMPT=$P$G
```

You can use the SET command to create an environment entry and assign a value to it, as follows:

```
C:\> SET SHOW_FILE=\AUTOEXEC.BAT
```

Then you can use the SET command to display the new environment entry as shown at the top of the following page.

```
C:\> SET
COMSPEC=C:\DOS\COMMAND.COM
PATH=C:\DOS
PROMPT $P$G
SHOW_FILE=\AUTOEXEC.BAT
```

When you run SHOWFILE.BAT, MS-DOS replaces the SHOW_FILE
named parameter with the corresponding environment entry—in this
case, AUTOEXEC.BAT—and displays the file's contents.

To remove an environment entry, use the SET command as follows:

```
C:\> SET SHOW_FILE=
```

Be sure to include the ending equal sign. In this case MS-DOS removes
the SHOW_FILE entry, and the contents of the environment are once
again this:

```
C:\> SET
COMSPEC=C:\DOS\COMMAND.COM
PATH=C:\DOS
PROMPT=$P$G
```

If you run the SHOWFILE.BAT batch file again, MS-DOS no longer
finds an environment entry that matches SHOW_FILE because the
named parameter contains the empty string. By using the IF command,
you can have your batch file test for the empty string and continue processing accordingly, as follows:

```
@ECHO OFF
IF "%SHOW_FILE%"=="" GOTO NO_PARAMETER
TYPE %SHOW_FILE% ¦ MORE
GOTO DONE
:NO_PARAMETER
ECHO The SHOW_FILE named parameter is
ECHO not defined. Use the SET command
ECHO to assign a filename to SHOW_FILE.
:DONE
```

Many people have trouble thinking of batch files that need named parameters, so let's look at one or two examples. First, suppose you have
a batch file that sometimes creates temporary files as it executes, and
you don't want MS-DOS to create the files in the current directory. For
example, the following batch file creates a temporary file called
SORTDIR.TMP:

```
DIR ¦ SORT > SORTDIR.TMP
PRINT SORTDIR.TMP
MORE < SORTDIR.TMP
DEL SORTDIR.TMP
```

If you run this batch file and end it using the Ctrl-C key combination before the DEL command completes execution, the SORTDIR.TMP file
remains in the current directory. As an alternative, you could create a
TEMPDIR directory to store the temporary files and then reference that
directory throughout the batch file, as follows:

```
DIR : SORT > \TEMPDIR\SORTDIR.TMP
PRINT \TEMPDIR\SORTDIR.TMP
MORE < \TEMPDIR\SORTDIR.TMP
DEL \TEMPDIR\SORTDIR.TMP
```

The problem with this method is that it forces all users to create a TEMP
DIR directory to hold the temporary files.

The following batch file, NAMEDTMP.BAT, uses a named parameter
to solve the problem of where to place temporary files:

```
DIR : SORT > %TEMPDIR%SORTDIR.TMP
PRINT %TEMPDIR%SORTDIR.TMP
MORE < %TEMPDIR%SORTDIR.TMP
DEL %TEMPDIR%SORTDIR.TMP
```

When MS-DOS encounters the %TEMPDIR% named parameter, it
searches the environment for a corresponding entry. If no such entry exists, MS-DOS assigns an empty string to %TEMPDIR% and creates the
SORTDIR.TMP file in the current directory. If you create an environment entry such as the following before running NAMEDTMP.BAT,
MS-DOS uses the named parameter to create the SORTDIR.TMP file
in the current directory of drive D:

```
C:\> SET TEMPDIR=D:
```

To specify a directory called DATA on drive D, you would use this:

```
C:\> SET TEMPDIR=D:\DATA\
```

This batch file handles the needs of all potential users of the batch file.
Users who don't care whether MS-DOS creates the file in the current
directory simply run the batch file without issuing a SET command to
define TEMPDIR. Users who want MS-DOS to create the file in a
specific directory, such as one that is on a fast RAM drive, simply use
SET to assign an appropriate drive, subdirectory, or both to the named
parameter.

As discussed earlier, the PATH= entry defines the list of subdirectories
that MS-DOS searches for external commands. Most people define
PATH= using the PATH command in AUTOEXEC.BAT. When you install an application, its installation program often adds the application's

newly created directory to the PATH command in AUTOEXEC.BAT. Assume, for this example, that the AUTOEXEC.BAT file contains the following commands:

```
@ECHO OFF
PRINT /D:LPT1 /Q:32
PATH C:\DOS
SET PROMPT=$P$G
```

Next assume that the installation program wants to add the C:\UTIL directory to the PATH command. The installation program will not change the following entry:

```
PATH C:\DOS
```

Instead the installation program can add this entry to the end of the batch file:

```
SET PATH=%PATH%;C:\UTIL
```

This entry takes advantage of the fact that the PATH command creates an MS-DOS environment entry, which you can use as a named parameter.

To better understand how this processing works, create a batch file named MYPATH.BAT that contains these commands:

```
@ECHO OFF
SET MYPATH=C:\DOS
ECHO Original entry is %MYPATH%
ECHO Appending C:\UTIL to %MYPATH%
SET MYPATH=%MYPATH%;C:\UTIL
ECHO Complete entry is %MYPATH%
```

When you run this batch file, MS-DOS displays the following:

```
Original entry is C:\DOS
Appending C:\UTIL to C:\DOS
Complete entry is C:\DOS;C:\UTIL
```

As you can see, the batch file creates the entry C:\DOS;C:\UTIL, as you intended.

Several of the batch files that we will examine throughout the remainder of this book will use MS-DOS named parameters.

RUNNING ONE BATCH FILE FROM WITHIN ANOTHER

All the programs executed by the batch files we have created so far have been either EXE or COM files. If you want one batch file to run another batch file (and continue executing the first batch file when the second completes), you need to use either the CALL command or the COMMAND /C command, depending on your version of MS-DOS.

To understand why your batch file cannot execute a second batch file simply by calling the name of the batch file as you would an MS-DOS command or a program, let's create a simple batch file named VER-VOL.BAT that contains these commands:

```
VER
VOL
```

Next create a batch file named PRIMARY.BAT that contains these commands:

```
DATE
VERVOL
TIME
```

PRIMARY.BAT runs the VERVOL.BAT batch file by referencing the batch file's name. When you run the PRIMARY.BAT batch file, MS-DOS first executes the DATE command and displays the following:

```
C:\> PRIMARY

C:\> DATE
Current date is Thu 04-07-1994
Enter new date (mm-dd-yy):
```

If you press Enter (leaving the date unchanged), MS-DOS runs the second batch file, VERVOL.BAT. As MS-DOS executes this batch file, MS-DOS displays the following:

```
C:\> PRIMARY

C:\> DATE
Current date is Thu 04-07-1994
Enter new date (mm-dd-yy):

C:\> VERVOL

C:\> VER

MS-DOS version 6.20


C:\> VOL

 Volume in drive C is DOS 6 DISK
 Volume Serial Number is 3921-18D3

C:\>
```

When the VERVOL.BAT batch file completes execution, MS-DOS does not execute the TIME command, the last command in PRIMARY.BAT. To return to PRIMARY.BAT after VERVOL.BAT completes execution, you must use either the CALL or COMMAND /C command to run the second batch file.

If you are using MS-DOS version 3.3 or later, you use the CALL command to execute the commands in a second batch file and then return to the next command in the first batch file. The format of the CALL command is as follows:

CALL BatchFile [parameters]

The parameters are the optional values that MS-DOS assigns to the %1 through %9 variables. If you are using MS-DOS version 3.3 or later, you can change the PRIMARY.BAT batch file to this:

```
DATE
CALL VERVOL
TIME
```

CALL Batch-File Command

Function:

Allows one batch file to run another batch file, followed by a return to the initial batch file.

Format:

CALL BatchFile [parameters]

Notes:

If you run one batch file from within another without using a CALL or COMMAND /C command (discussed in this chapter), MS-DOS executes commands only until the second batch file completes execution. If you run the second batch file from the middle of the first batch file, the commands in the first batch file that follow the command that invokes the second batch file will never execute. When the second batch file ends, the execution of all batch-file commands ends.

If you are using MS-DOS version 3.3 or later, you can use the CALL command to run one batch file from within another and then return to the initial batch file. Simply place the name of the second batch file on the CALL command line, along with any batch-file parameters.

When you run this batch file, MS-DOS again executes the DATE command. As before, press Enter to leave the system date unchanged. MS-DOS then executes the CALL command, which in turn runs the VERVOL.BAT batch file. When VERVOL.BAT completes execution, MS-DOS executes the next command in·PRIMARY.BAT, the TIME command. As a result, MS-DOS displays the following:

```
C:\> PRIMARY

C:\> DATE
Current date is Thu 04-07-1994
Enter new date (mm-dd-yy):

C:\> CALL VERVOL

C:\> VER

MS-DOS version 6.20
```

(continued)

Example:

This batch file uses the CALL command to run a second batch file named NESTED.BAT:

```
VER
CALL NESTED
VOL
```

In this case, NESTED.BAT contains these commands:

```
DATE
TIME
```

If you remove the CALL command from the first batch file, the following remain:

```
VER
NESTED
VOL
```

MS-DOS never executes the VOL command. When NESTED.BAT completes execution, MS-DOS stops executing batch-file commands and returns to the command prompt.

```
C:\> VOL

Volume in drive C is DOS 6 DISK
Volume Serial Number is 3921-18D3

C:\> TIME
Current time is 1:54:09.09p
Enter new time:

C:\>
```

As you can see, the CALL command allows a batch file to successfully run a second batch file and then return to the first file to execute the remaining commands.

If you are using an MS-DOS version earlier than 3.3, you must use COMMAND /C to run a second batch file. (You can also use this command in later versions.) The COMMAND.COM file contains the

---

COMMAND /C Batch-File Command

Function:

Allows one batch file to run another batch file, followed by a return to the initial batch file.

Format:

COMMAND /C BatchFile [parameters]

Notes:

If you run one batch file from within another without using a CALL or COMMAND /C command, MS-DOS executes commands only until the second batch file completes execution. If you run the second batch file from the middle of the first batch file, the commands in the first batch file that follow the command that invokes the second batch file will never execute. When the second batch file ends, the execution of all batch-file commands ends.

If you are using MS-DOS version 3.2 or earlier, you can use the COMMAND /C command to run one batch file from within another and then return to the initial batch file. Simply place the name of the second batch file on the COMMAND /C command line, along with any batch-file parameters.

MS-DOS command-line processor, which executes commands as you type them at the command prompt, as well as the commands in a batch file. If you are using an MS-DOS version earlier than 3.3, change the PRIMARY.BAT batch file so that it contains the following:

```
DATE
COMMAND /C VERVOL
TIME
```

Be sure that the COMMAND.COM file resides in the current directory or in a directory referenced in the PATH statement.

When you run the batch file, MS-DOS executes the DATE command. As before, press Enter to leave the system date unchanged. The batch file continues processing, using COMMAND /C to run the VER-VOL.BAT batch file. When VERVOL.BAT completes execution, MS-DOS executes the TIME command in the PRIMARY.BAT batch file.

Example:

This batch file uses COMMAND /C to run a second batch file named NESTED.BAT:

```
VER
COMMAND /C NESTED
VOL
```

In this case, NESTED.BAT contains these commands:

```
DATE
TIME
```

If you remove the COMMAND /C command from the first batch file, the following commands remain:

```
VER
NESTED
VOL
```

MS-DOS never executes the VOL command. When NESTED.BAT completes execution, MS-DOS stops executing batch-file commands and returns to the command prompt.

NOTE: *You can use the COMMAND command without any parameters in all versions of MS-DOS to load a second command processor. You must use the EXIT command to return to batch-file processing.*

COMMAND /C directs MS-DOS to load a second command processor into memory. The /C tells MS-DOS to keep the command processor in memory only until the command that follows has been executed. In this case, the second command processor remains in memory just long enough to execute the commands in the VERVOL.BAT batch file. When the batch file completes execution, MS-DOS removes the second command processor from memory and continues execution of the commands in the PRIMARY.BAT batch file.

USING A SECOND COMMAND PROCESSOR

As your batch files increase in complexity, you might want to display a list of menu options, each of which results in the execution of a different MS-DOS command. One of the options might temporarily suspend the batch file's execution so that the user can execute commands from the command prompt. The MS-DOS COMMAND command lets your batch files do exactly that.

The next batch file, USEDOS.BAT, contains these commands:

```
@ECHO OFF
ECHO In batch file, about to access command prompt
COMMAND
ECHO Back in batch file
```

When MS-DOS encounters COMMAND, MS-DOS loads a second command processor into memory, which displays a command prompt that allows you to execute MS-DOS commands. Any changes you make to the environment entries in the second command processor remain in effect only until you quit that command processor. When you no longer want to execute MS-DOS commands, you use the EXIT command to quit the second command processor.

If the COMMAND.COM file resides in the current directory or in a directory that is on the search path, when you run the USEDOS.BAT batch file, MS-DOS displays the following:

```
C:\> USEDOS

In batch file, about to access command prompt


MICROSOFT(R) MS-DOS(R) Version 6.20
            (C)Copyright Microsoft Corp 1981-1993.

C:\>
```

MS-DOS has loaded a second command processor, allowing you to issue commands at the command prompt. In this case, issue the DATE command to display the current system date. To return control to the batch file, issue the EXIT command. Your screen now looks like this:

```
C:\> USEDOS
In batch file, about to access command prompt


MICROSOFT(R) MS-DOS(R) Version 6.20
          (C)Copyright Microsoft Corp 1981-1993.

C:\> DATE
Current date is Thu 04-07-1994
Enter new date (mm-dd-yy):

C:\> EXIT
Back in batch file

C:\>
```

When the EXIT command completes execution, MS-DOS returns control to the batch file, which continues its execution.

HANDLING MORE THAN NINE PARAMETERS WITH SHIFT

As you have learned, the %1 through %9 batch-file parameters let you pass nine values to your batch files. Being able to pass values to batch files in this manner increases their flexibility. It also enables them to support many more applications than batch files that don't support parameter processing. Even so, for some uses the nine-parameter restriction can still cause problems. In such situations, the SHIFT command provides a solution.

The primary purpose of the SHIFT command is to allow batch files to access more than nine batch parameters. When MS-DOS encounters SHIFT in a batch file, it moves each batch parameter value one position to the left, assigning the value of %1 to the %0 parameter, the value of %2 to %1, and so on. If your command line contains more than nine parameters, SHIFT assigns the tenth one to %9; otherwise, SHIFT assigns the empty string to %9. As an example, let's consider the batch file ONESHIFT.BAT, shown on the following page.

```
@ECHO OFF
CLS
ECHO %0 %1 %2 %3 %4 %5 %6 %7 %8 %9
SHIFT
ECHO %0 %1 %2 %3 %4 %5 %6 %7 %8 %9
```

For example, you can run this batch file by typing the following:

```
C:\> ONESHIFT A B C
```

MS-DOS then clears the screen and displays this:

```
ONESHIFT A B C
A B C
```

Additionally, you can run this batch file with more than nine parameters by typing the following:

```
C:\> ONESHIFT 1 2 3 4 5 6 7 8 9 10 11
```

SHIFT Batch-File Command

Function:

Shifts each batch-file parameter value one parameter to the left. MS-DOS assigns the value of %1 to %0, the value of %2 to %1, and so on.

Format:

SHIFT

Notes:

MS-DOS supports the batch parameters %0 through %9. If your command line contains more than nine parameters, you can use the SHIFT command to access the additional parameters. For example, you can run a batch file named SHIFTTST.BAT with this command line:

```
C:\> SHIFTTST A B C D
```

The batch parameters are then as follows:

%0 contains SHIFTTST
%1 contains A
%2 contains B
%3 contains C
%4 contains D
%5 contains "" (empty string)

If the batch file contains a SHIFT command, MS-DOS shifts each parameter, with this result:

MS-DOS then displays this:

```
ONESHIFT 1 2 3 4 5 6 7 8 9
1 2 3 4 5 6 7 8 9 10
```

Notice that SHIFT assigns the value 10 to the %9 parameter. Pictorially, this SHIFT operation becomes the following:

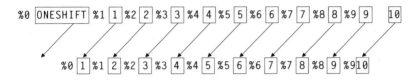

%0 contains A
%1 contains B
%2 contains C
%3 contains D
%4 contains "" (empty string)
%5 contains "" (empty string)

If the command line contains more than nine parameters, SHIFT assigns the tenth parameter to %9. The next iteration assigns the eleventh parameter to %9; and so on. When no parameters remain, SHIFT assigns an empty string to %9.

Example:

The following batch file uses SHIFT to display all the batch-file parameters typed on the command line:

```
:REPEAT
If "%1"=="" GOTO NO_MORE
ECHO %1
SHIFT
GOTO REPEAT
:NO_MORE
```

The batch file simply loops, displaying the current value of %1. As long as %1 is not the empty string, the loop continues, and a new parameter value is shifted into %1.

The next batch file, TWOSHIFT.BAT, uses the SHIFT command twice:

```
@ECHO OFF
CLS
ECHO %0 %1 %2 %3 %4 %5 %6 %7 %8 %9
SHIFT
ECHO %0 %1 %2 %3 %4 %5 %6 %7 %8 %9
SHIFT
ECHO %0 %1 %2 %3 %4 %5 %6 %7 %8 %9
```

You can run the batch file by typing this:

```
C:\> TWOSHIFT A B C
```

MS-DOS clears the screen and displays this:

```
TWOSHIFT A B C
A B C
B C
```

As before, you can run the batch file with more than nine batch parameters by typing the following:

```
C:\> TWOSHIFT 1 2 3 4 5 6 7 8 9 10 11
```

MS-DOS then clears the screen and displays this:

```
TWOSHIFT 1 2 3 4 5 6 7 8 9
1 2 3 4 5 6 7 8 9 10
2 3 4 5 6 7 8 9 10 11
```

Keep in mind that when SHIFT no longer has values to assign to %9, SHIFT assigns the empty string to %9. By testing for the empty string, you can create the following batch file, SHIFT_IT.BAT, which uses the GOTO command to loop through all the command-line parameters and the ECHO command to display each on its own line:

```
@ECHO OFF
:REPEAT
ECHO %0
SHIFT
IF NOT "%0"=="" GOTO REPEAT
```

You can run the batch file as follows:

```
C:\> SHIFT_IT ONE TWO THREE
```

MS-DOS then displays this:

```
SHIFT_IT
ONE
TWO
THREE
```

When the batch file first begins execution, %0 contains the name of the batch file. When the batch file executes the SHIFT command, MS-DOS assigns the word *ONE* to %0. Because %0 is not equal to the empty string, the batch file issues the GOTO command, and this process repeats. After the fourth SHIFT command, %0 contains the empty string, and the batch file ends.

Using this same technique, you can change the SHIFT_IT.BAT batch file slightly to create a batch file named D.BAT that enhances the DIR command:

```
@ECHO OFF
:REPEAT
DIR %1
SHIFT
IF NOT "%1"=="" GOTO REPEAT
```

You can now run the batch file with the following command line:

```
C:\> D \*.BAT \BAT \UTILS\*.BAT
```

The batch file then displays successive directory listings for the specified file and directory. In this case, it displays any files with the BAT extension in the root directory (*.BAT), followed by all files in the BAT directory and, finally, any BAT files in the \UTILS directory. You can replace the line

```
DIR %1
```

with

```
FOR %%A IN (%1) DO TYPE %%A
```

The batch file then uses the TYPE command to display each of the files you specify in the command line.

BATCH-FILE PROBLEMS

This section takes a look at several problems you might encounter when you run your batch files. Take time to read each of the following discussions closely. They may save you considerable time and effort as you try to determine why a batch file doesn't work properly.

Bad command or file name Error Message

If your batch file displays the following message, a command within the batch file is invalid:

```
Bad command or file name
```

The quickest way to determine which command is responsible for the error message is to remove ECHO OFF so that MS-DOS displays each command name as the batch file executes. The incorrect command name appears on your screen immediately before the error message. For example, the following batch file, BADCMD.BAT, contains an invalid MS-DOS command:

```
VER
XYZ12345
VOL
```

When you run this batch file, MS-DOS displays this:

```
C:\> VER
MS-DOS version 6.20


C:\> XYZ12345
Bad command or file name

C:\> VOL

 Volume in drive C is DOS 6 DISK
 Volume Serial Number is 3921-18D3

C:\>
```

Notice that MS-DOS displayed the error message immediately following the XYZ12345 command.

When a batch file contains an invalid command, MS-DOS displays the error message and continues execution with the next command. Sometimes the command is a *valid* MS-DOS command—yet MS-DOS still issues the *Bad command or file name* error message when MS-DOS encounters the command. In such cases, the problem is not the command name but rather where MS-DOS is searching on your hard disk for the command.

Remember: MS-DOS defines commands as either internal or external. Internal commands (such as TYPE, DATE, CLS, and VER) always reside in your computer's memory after MS-DOS starts. External commands (such as CHOICE and FORMAT) reside on disk. To execute an external command, MS-DOS must first find the command on disk and load the command into memory. If the command does not reside in the current directory, in the specified directory, or on the search path, MS-DOS displays the *Bad command or file name* error message simply because it cannot locate the file. As discussed earlier, the PATH command specifies where MS-DOS should search for commands. If you know that the command generating the *Bad command or file name* error message is valid, check that the command's directory is on the search path so that MS-DOS can locate the command.

NOTE: *You cannot invoke a DOSKEY macro from within a batch file. (DOSKEY is the topic of the next chapter.) If you do invoke a macro from a batch file, MS-DOS displays* Bad command or file name.

If you get a *Bad command or file name* error message when you know all the commands in your batch file are valid and can be successfully located, your word processor has probably embedded a strange character that MS-DOS cannot understand in the batch file. If you are creating your batch files with a word processor, be sure you save the file in ASCII (text) format.

File not found Error Message

If your batch file displays the following message, the commands in your batch file are valid, but MS-DOS cannot locate a file that one of the commands is trying to use:

```
File not found
```

For example, the next batch file, BADFILE.BAT, contains the following command:

```
TYPE 12345678.XYZ
```

When you run this batch file, MS-DOS displays this:

```
File not found-12345678.XYZ

C:\>
```

Although MS-DOS successfully executed the TYPE command, TYPE could not locate the file 12345678.XYZ. By using the IF EXIST command with the proper path, your batch files can test to ensure that a file exists before trying to use the file.

NOTE: *MS-DOS searches the directories specified in the PATH command for commands, not for files. Either a file must be in the current directory or the complete path to the file must be specified.*

Missing or Poorly Named Batch Labels

As you already know, the GOTO command lets your batch files branch from one location within the file to another. When MS-DOS encounters a GOTO command, it searches the batch file for the specified label. If MS-DOS encounters the label, it continues batch-file execution with the command that immediately follows the label. If the label does not exist, MS-DOS stops executing the batch file and displays this message:

```
Label not found
```

·If this error occurs, be sure that your batch file contains the label, that the label is spelled correctly, and that it is preceded by a colon. (Remember that you shouldn't use the colon when referencing the label in the GOTO command.) The following batch file, NOLABEL.BAT, demonstrates how MS-DOS immediately stops batch-file execution when a label is invalid:

```
GOTO DONE
VER
VOL
```

When you run this batch file, MS-DOS displays the following without executing either the VER or VOL command:

```
Label not found
```

Keep in mind that MS-DOS uses only the first eight letters of a label's name. If MS-DOS cannot distinguish between two labels, it uses the first label it encounters. The next batch file, 2LABELS.BAT, uses the labels *BatchLabelOne* and *BatchLabelTwo*:

```
:BatchLabelOne
VER
GOTO BatchLabelTwo
VOL
:BatchLabelTwo
```

Because the first eight letters of the labels' names are the same, MS-DOS considers the labels to be identical. When you run this batch file, MS-DOS repeatedly displays the current version number until you use the Ctrl-C key combination to end the command.

I/O REDIRECTION AND BATCH-FILE CONFLICTS

As you know, the MS-DOS output (>) and append (>>) redirection operators let you redirect a command's output to a file or to a device such as the printer. However, you can't redirect a batch file's output. For example, if you have a batch file name DIRSORT.BAT, you cannot use the following command to redirect the batch file's output to the printer:

```
C:\> DIRSORT > PRN
```

If you want to redirect the batch file's output, you must individually redirect the output of each batch-file command.

The IF Command's I/O Redirection Restrictions

Most complex batch files make extensive use of the IF command, but the pipe (¦) I/O redirection operator doesn't work in IF commands. If you need to redirect output from one MS-DOS command to another in response to an IF command, first perform the necessary test, and then branch to a location within the batch file where the redirection can be performed, as shown here:

```
IF "%1"=="SORT" GOTO SORT
REM Other commands here
:SORT
DIR ¦ SORT
```

I/O Redirection and IF EXIST

Your batch files will often need to test whether a specific file exists and perform some operation if it doesn't. For example, the following command tests whether the IO_TEST.DAT file exists and, if it doesn't, redirects the output of the DIR command to the OTEST.DAT file:

```
IF NOT EXIST IO_TEST.DAT DIR > IO_TEST.DAT
```

The command appears very straightforward. You would think that if the IO_TEST.DAT file didn't exist, the batch file would create it, assigning to it the list of files in the current directory; otherwise, the batch file would do nothing. Unfortunately, that's not how MS-DOS works. When the command specified in an IF command uses redirection to a file, MS-DOS first opens that file in anticipation of the subsequent output. Then MS-DOS performs the IF command's test—in this case, testing whether the IO_TEST.DAT file exists. Because MS-DOS just created the file, it does exist, and the IF NOT EXIST command always fails. After the command executes, the IO_TEST.DAT file exists but is empty.

To correct this problem, replace the command line with an IF...GOTO statement that performs the test to determine whether the file exists and, if it doesn't, branches to the correct location, as shown here:

```
IF NOT EXIST IO_TEST.DAT GOTO NO_FILE
REM Other commands here
:NO_FILE
DIR > IO_TEST.DAT
```

CHAPTER 7

Using DOSKEY and Defining DOSKEY Macros

RECALLING COMMANDS TO THE COMMAND LINE

As you have learned, MS-DOS batch files can save time and reduce keystrokes. If you are using MS-DOS version 5 or later, you can also use the powerful DOSKEY command to simplify your work. After you invoke DOSKEY, MS-DOS builds a list of the names of each command executed from the command prompt. Using the arrow keys on your keyboard, you can quickly move through this list, repeating or slightly modifying previously entered commands.

To better understand this process, invoke DOSKEY as shown here:

```
C:\> DOSKEY
DOSKEY installed.
```

If you don't see the *DOSKEY installed* message, DOSKEY is already installed. In that case, enter the DOSKEY /REINSTALL command to clear any saved commands and prepare for this exercise.

Next invoke the CLS, VER, and VOL commands one after another. As each command executes, MS-DOS records the command's name in the command list. You can display the list of buffered command names by invoking DOSKEY with the /HISTORY (or /H) switch. In this case, DOSKEY displays the commands CLS, VER, and VOL, as shown here:

```
C:\> DOSKEY /HISTORY
CLS
VER
VOL
DOSKEY /HISTORY

C:\>
```

You can also press F7 as a shortcut for displaying the command history. When you display the commands using F7, DOSKEY precedes each command name with a number that reflects the command's relative position in the list, like this:

```
1: CLS
2: VER
3: VOL
4: DOSKEY /HISTORY
```

If you press the F9 key, DOSKEY prompts you to enter the line number of the desired command:

```
C:\> Line number:
```

If you type *1* and press Enter, DOSKEY displays CLS on the current command line; if you type *2*, DOSKEY displays VER; and so on.

You can also use the following keys to recall commands to the command line:

Key	Action
Up arrow	Recalls the command issued immediately before the currently displayed command.
Down arrow	Recalls the command issued immediately after the currently displayed command.
PgUp	Recalls the oldest command in the list.
PgDn	Recalls the newest command in the list.

Experiment with the arrow keys, cycling through the CLS, VER, and VOL commands.

Each time you recall a command, MS-DOS places the cursor at the end of the command so that you can execute the command quickly by pressing Enter. If you want to change the command before executing it, MS-DOS lets you use the following editing keys to move to the proper location:

Key	Action
Left arrow	Moves the cursor one position to the left without deleting the character. (Note: If DOSKEY is not installed, the character is deleted.)
Right arrow	Moves the cursor one position to the right. (Note: If starting from a blank command line, the next character from the previous command is displayed.)
Ctrl-Left arrow	Moves the cursor one word to the left.

Key	Action
Ctrl-Right arrow	Moves the cursor one word to the right. (Note: If starting from a blank command line, the next word from the previous command is displayed.)
Home	Moves the cursor to the start of the command.
End	Moves the cursor to the end of the command.
Esc	Clears the command from the command line.

You can use these keys to edit the command line:

Key	Action
Backspace	Deletes the character immediately to the left of the cursor.
Delete	Deletes the character at the cursor.
Insert	Toggles between insert and overstrike mode.

The use of the Insert key requires a bit of explanation. In the default mode, new characters replace (overstrike) the characters already on the command line. When you press Insert, the cursor changes from an underscore to a square, DOSKEY switches to insert mode, and the new characters are inserted into the text. (The existing characters are moved to the right.) The insert mode is reset to overstrike mode when you press Enter.

This process can be changed by specifying the /INSERT switch when starting (or reinstalling) DOSKEY. If you start DOSKEY with the /INSERT switch, insert mode becomes the default. Pressing Insert still causes the cursor to change to a square, but now the new characters replace the existing characters. (The default setting is the equivalent of using the /OVERSTRIKE switch.)

MS-DOS always stores the previous command as a *command template*. It is often easier to create a new command line by editing an old one. You can use these standard command editing keys to work with the command as stored in the command template:

Key	Action
F1	Copies one character from the previous command to the current command line.
F2	Copies characters from the previous command up to, but not including, the first occurrence of the character you type after pressing F2.
F3	Copies the remainder (from the current character to the end) of the previous command to the current command line.

(continued)

(continued)

Key	Action
F4	Deletes from the previous command all the characters up to, but not including, the first occurrence of the character you type after pressing F4. You can then display the remaining portion of the command by using F1, F2, or F3. You start with a blank command line and build the new command using characters from the previous command.
F5	Makes the currently displayed command the command template without executing the command and clears the current command line. (Note: Without DOSKEY loaded, F5 acts like the Esc key.)

As you work with MS-DOS, the ability to quickly repeat previous commands using DOSKEY's command-recall capability will save you considerable time and typing.

CREATING DOSKEY MACROS

In addition to letting you quickly recall previous commands, DOSKEY allows you to create macros, which are similar to simple batch files. Like batch files, macros contain one or more commands, which MS-DOS associates with the macro name. Unlike batch files which have the BAT extension and reside on disk, macros reside in your computer's fast electronic RAM and are lost when you turn off your computer.

NOTE: *To make your most commonly used macros available each time your system starts, you can place the DOSKEY commands that define the macros in your AUTOEXEC.BAT file.*

To create a macro, you use the DOSKEY command followed by the macro's name, an equal sign, and the commands that make up the macro. If a macro contains more than one command, you use the $T (or $t) metacharacter to separate them.

The following DOSKEY command creates a macro named CLSVV that clears your screen and then executes the VER and VOL commands:

```
C:\> DOSKEY CLSVV=CLS $T VER $T VOL
```

You must specify the macro name (in this case, CLSVV), followed by the equal sign. Notice that the macro uses $T to separate commands. To execute this macro, simply type the macro name at the command prompt and press Enter, like this:

```
C:\> CLSVV
```

As you have seen in previous chapters, the %1 through %9 batch-file parameters greatly increase the capabilities of your batch files. DOSKEY macros also support command-line parameters. In the case of macros, however, you access the parameters using the symbols $1 through $9. The following macro, SHOWEM, uses these symbols to display its command-line parameters:

```
C:\> DOSKEY SHOWEM=ECHO $1 $2 $3 $4 $5 $6 $7 $8 $9
```

If you invoke SHOWEM with the letters A, B, and C, your screen displays the following:

```
C:\> SHOWEM A B C
C:\> ECHO A B C
A B C
```

DOSKEY macros don't support the SHIFT command that moves parameters one position to the left. Instead, DOSKEY macros support the $* metacharacter, which MS-DOS replaces with the macro's command line minus the macro name. The following command creates a macro named SHOWIT that displays all of its parameters using $*:

```
C:\> DOSKEY SHOWIT=ECHO $*
```

Note that, like MS-DOS batch files, the macro displays the name of the command as the command executes. However, you cannot use ECHO OFF to disable the macro command-name display the way you can with batch files.

Many people create a directory using MD (or MKDIR) and then immediately use CD (or CHDIR) to make that directory the current directory. The following macro, MDCD, creates the specified directory and immediately makes that directory the current directory:

```
C:\> DOSKEY MDCD=MKDIR $1 $T CHDIR $1
```

To use the macro to create a directory called TEST and make it the current directory, you run the macro like this:

```
C:\> MDCD TEST
```

If you create a macro with the same name as an existing macro, DOSKEY overwrites the existing macro. For example, the following command changes the SHOWEM macro to display each parameter on its own line:

```
C:\> DOSKEY SHOWEM=FOR %I IN ($*) DO ECHO %I
```

You may notice that we used the command-line form of the FOR statement (%I) rather than the batch-file form (%%I). DOSKEY always works with commands as though they were entered from the command line. DOSKEY macros also support the MS-DOS I/O redirection operators. However, if you use the standard symbols (>, <, and ┆), the output from the DOSKEY command is redirected. To represent the redirection operators in macros, use the following symbols:

Operator	Function
$G or $g	Output redirection operator (>)
$L or $l	Input redirection operator (<)
$B or $b	Pipe redirection operator (┆)

The following macro, FINDNOTE, uses the FIND command to search through the README.TXT file included with MS-DOS version 6. It pipes the information from the FIND command through MORE to allow you to read the display one screen at a time.

DOSKEY Command

Function:

Lets you recall and edit previously issued commands using your keyboard's arrow keys. Also lets you define macros containing one or more MS-DOS commands.

Format:

[drive:][path]DOSKEY [/REINSTALL]
[/BUFSIZE=BufferSize][/MACROS ┆ /M][/HISTORY ┆ /H]
[/INSERT ┆ /OVERSTRIKE][MacroName=MacroText]

Notes:

DOSKEY is a memory-resident software program.

The /REINSTALL switch directs DOSKEY to clear all commands and macros from the buffer and to install a new version of itself in memory.

DOSKEY stores your commands and macros in a buffer in memory. You can use the /BUFSIZE=BufferSize switch to specify the size of this buffer the first time you invoke DOSKEY or when you use the /RE-INSTALL switch. The default buffer size is 1024 bytes. If you are creating a large number of macros, you might want to increase the buffer size to 4096 bytes.

```
DOSKEY FINDNOTE=FIND $1 \DOS\README.TXT /I $B MORE
```

When you run FINDNOTE, you can specify a single word (enclosed in quotes) for the search; for example:

```
FINDNOTE "MemMaker"
```

The macro is expanded to this:

```
FIND "MemMaker" \DOS\README.TXT /I ¦ MORE
```

Note that the $B is replaced with the pipe symbol. (The /I switch is used to configure FIND to ignore case when searching for matches.)

The next example, FINDNAME, uses two parameters, one specifying the string and the other the filename. The output from the FIND command is sorted and then directed to the printer. This file is designed to extract lines containing the string from an unsorted file and produce a sorted listing. The macro definition for FINDNAME is this:

```
DOSKEY FINDNAME=FIND "$1" $2 /I $B SORT $G PRN
```

The DOSKEY /MACROS switch directs DOSKEY to display the macros currently in memory. The /HISTORY switch directs DOSKEY to display the list of the commands in the buffer.

The /INSERT switch directs MS-DOS to set insert mode so that new typing inserts characters in the line. The /OVERSTRIKE switch directs MS-DOS to replace old characters with new ones. The Insert key can be used to temporarily switch modes.

To create a macro, specify its name, followed by an equal sign and the commands that make up the macro, all on one line. Separate commands with the $T or $t metacharacter.

Examples:

The following command directs DOSKEY to display both the contents of the current command buffer and any defined macros:

```
C:\> DOSKEY /HISTORY /MACROS
```

The following DOSKEY command creates a macro named CK that abbreviates the MS-DOS CHKDSK command:

```
C:\> DOSKEY CK=CHKDSK
```

In the previous example, the quotation marks have been placed around the variable, so they do not need to be entered at the command line. To use this command, you enter the following:

```
FINDNAME Joe BIRTHDAY.DAT
```

This then becomes the following:

```
FIND "Joe" BIRTHDAY.DAT /I ¦ SORT > PRN
```

Then a sorted list of everybody with "Joe" as part of their name would be printed.

The /MACROS (or /M) switch directs DOSKEY to display its current list of macros. Assuming that you have created the macros we've discussed, DOSKEY displays the following:

```
C:\> DOSKEY /M
CLSVV=CLS $T VER $T VOL
SHOWIT=ECHO $*
MDCD=MKDIR $1 $T CHDIR $1
SHOWEM=FOR %I IN ($*) DO ECHO %I
FINDNOTE=FIND $1 \DOS\APPNOTES.TXT /I $B MORE
FINDNAME=FIND "$1" $2 /I $B SORT $G PRN

C:\>
```

What Macros Can't Do

As mentioned earlier, macros are similar but not identical to batch files. For example, macros don't allow you to use the ECHO OFF command to disable command-name display. Likewise, you cannot use the GOTO command within a macro to branch from one location to another. MS-DOS lets you run a batch file from within a macro, but you cannot run a macro from within a batch file or run one macro from within another. You can, however, use a batch file to define one or more macros. Batch files can be interrupted by pressing Ctrl-C. In a macro, Ctrl-C stops only the current command. Therefore, you must press the Ctrl-C keyboard combination for each of the commands in the macro.

Redefining MS-DOS Commands

As you know, you should not assign the name of an internal or external MS-DOS command to a batch file. However, there may be times when you want to assign the name of an MS-DOS command to a macro. When you issue commands from the command prompt, MS-DOS first checks whether the command matches a DOSKEY macro. If it doesn't,

MS-DOS checks whether the command is an internal command, and then determines whether the command is an external command or batch file. By assigning a macro the same name as an MS-DOS command, you can effectively redefine or disable the command.

For example, the following DOSKEY command creates a macro named FORMAT that always copies the system files to a disk after formatting it:

```
C:\> DOSKEY FORMAT=FORMAT /S $*
```

Each time you use this FORMAT macro to format a disk, the $* is replaced with the options you specify (such as the drive to format). For example, you can type the following:

```
FORMAT A:
```

The DOSKEY macro then substitutes this:

```
FORMAT /S A:
```

The macro replaces the standard FORMAT command and inserts the desired switch. The disadvantage to this revision is that the FORMAT command returns an error if a switch is repeated. So if you type *FORMAT /S a:*, MS-DOS returns an error.

This use of DOSKEY allows you to customize any MS-DOS command (much like the DIR command can be customized with the DIRCMD environment entry). You can also use this feature to disable an MS-DOS command. To disable the FORMAT command, use the following macro:

```
DOSKEY FORMAT=CLS $T ECHO That Command Is Not Available
```

Whenever you try to use the FORMAT command, the screen is cleared and MS-DOS displays the following:

```
ECHO That Command Is Not Available
That Command Is Not Available
```

There is no way to suppress the display of the ECHO command when working with macros.

Macros are ignored from within batch files because of the way MS-DOS handles them. Thus, if you created a batch file containing the FORMAT command, MS-DOS would find the normal command rather than the macro definition. Furthermore, if you specify on the command line the entire path to the command (\DOS\FORMAT), the original command is executed rather than the macro. Finally, placing a space before the command name always executes the MS-DOS command (rather than the macro).

Saving Disk Space Using DOSKEY Macros

Each time you create a file, MS-DOS allocates one or more disk storage units, called *clusters*, to hold the file's contents. On a typical hard disk, a cluster contains 4096 bytes. MS-DOS allocates at least one cluster for every file, regardless of the file's size. For example, assume you have a file that contains only 10 bytes. MS-DOS allocates one cluster to store the file. In the case of a 4096-byte cluster, 10 bytes are used and 4086 bytes are wasted. Obviously, the greater the number of small files on your disk, the larger the amount of wasted disk space.

Because MS-DOS stores DOSKEY macros in memory, not on disk, macros don't waste the disk space that would be consumed by small batch files. If you regularly use a set of DOSKEY macros, you can define the macros from within your AUTOEXEC.BAT file. By converting smaller batch files to macros, you can delete the batch files from your disk and free up considerable disk space.

Saving Macro Definitions in a File

If you have created several macros whose definitions you want to store in a file, redirect the output of the DOSKEY /MACROS commands to a file with the BAT extension, as shown here:

```
C:\> DOSKEY /MACROS > MACDEFS.BAT
```

DOSKEY then places a single-line entry for each of your macro definitions in the MACDEFS.BAT file. For example, if you had defined three macros—CP, PR, and CLSVV—they would now be listed in the MACDEFS.BAT file as follows:

```
CP=COPY $1 $2
PR=PRINT $*
CLSVV=CLS $T VER $T VOL
```

By editing the file to add the DOSKEY command in front of each entry, you can quickly create a batch file that defines your commonly used macros, as shown here:

```
DOSKEY CP=COPY $1 $2
DOSKEY PR=PRINT $*
DOSKEY CLSVV=CLS $T VER $T VOL
```

Building a Macro Library

In the same way that you can build a library of MS-DOS batch files, you can build a library of DOSKEY macros. This section examines a couple of simple macros you might want to add to your library.

Hiding and Unhiding Files

Beginning with MS-DOS version 5, you can use the ATTRIB command to change a file's hidden attribute. When this attribute is set, the file does not appear in directory listings, even though the file remains safely intact on your disk. When the hidden attribute is not set, the file appears in directory listings. The following DOSKEY macro, HIDE, sets a file's hidden attribute:

```
C:\> DOSKEY HIDE=ATTRIB +H $1
```

After you define the macro, you can hide a file as follows:

```
C:\> HIDE FILENAME.EXT
```

In a similar way, the UNHIDE macro removes the hidden attribute:

```
C:\> DOSKEY UNHIDE=ATTRIB -H $1
```

To unhide a file, run the macro with this command line:

```
C:\> UNHIDE FILENAME.EXT
```

There may be times when you need to view the names of the hidden files on your disk. The following macro, SHOWHIDE, displays a directory listing of only the hidden files on the current disk:

```
C:\> DOSKEY SHOWHIDE=DIR \*.* /A:H /S
```

Simplifying Disk-Format Operations

If you need to format a 360-KB disk in a 1.2-MB floppy-disk drive or a 720-KB disk in a 1.44-MB drive, you can use the following DOSKEY macros, MAKE360 and MAKE720, to make this process very easy:

```
C:\> DOSKEY MAKE360=FORMAT $1 /F:360
C:\> DOSKEY MAKE720=FORMAT $1 /F:720
```

To format a 360-KB floppy disk in drive A, you then invoke the MAKE360 macro as follows:

```
C:\> MAKE360 A:
```

CHAPTER 8

Enhancing Batch Files with ANSI.SYS

LOADING ANSI.SYS

This chapter takes a detailed look at the ANSI.SYS device driver, which you use to set screen colors, clear the screen, position the cursor on the screen so that your batch files can display their output in specific locations, and assign commands to function keys. As you will learn, using ANSI.SYS is not only fun but it also unleashes powerful capabilities within your batch files.

The ANSI.SYS device driver is stored in your DOS directory. The SYS file extension tells you that ANSI.SYS is a device driver. A *device driver* is a program used to control the system's communication with a device or a set of devices. In the case of ANSI.SYS, the device is the console. The console, or CON, is the keyboard (for input) and the screen (for output).

Before you can use ANSI.SYS, you must load it into memory. To load a device driver, you add a DEVICE= (or DEVICEHIGH=) entry to your CONFIG.SYS file. (You will recall that MS-DOS carries out the commands in CONFIG.SYS each time your system starts to configure the MS-DOS environment and MS-DOS's communication with devices.) For ANSI.SYS, your CONFIG.SYS entry is this:

```
DEVICE=C:\DOS\ANSI.SYS
```

If you are using MS-DOS version 5 or later and are using the upper memory area, you can load the ANSI.SYS device driver using the DEVICEHIGH= entry, as shown here:

```
DEVICEHIGH=C:\DOS\ANSI.SYS
```

After you add the entry to the CONFIG.SYS file, reboot your computer so that the change takes effect.

ANSI.SYS ESCAPE SEQUENCES

To use the ANSI.SYS-enhanced capabilities of your screen and keyboard from within your batch files, you must use either the PROMPT command or the ECHO command to send escape sequences that are interpreted by the device driver. An *escape sequence* is a unique character combination that begins with the ASCII escape character (ASCII 27). The ANSI.SYS device driver controls MS-DOS's communication with your screen and keyboard and supports several escape sequences that set your screen color, set the cursor position, or redefine keys on your keyboard. The PROMPT command offers the easiest way to experiment with ANSI escape sequences. With the PROMPT command, you can issue escape sequences either directly from the command line or from within a batch file.

The PROMPT command makes it easy to include the escape character in the escape sequence. The PROMPT command uses *metacharacters* (two-character combinations starting with the dollar sign) to indicate values that are to be inserted when the prompt is displayed. For example, the $p metacharacter represents the current drive and directory and the $g metacharacter represents the greater than symbol (>). These two characters combine to create the standard command prompt. To include an escape sequence with the PROMPT command, you use the $e metacharacter to represent the escape character. When the prompt is displayed, the escape character is substituted for $e. The instructions following the escape character are then interpreted by ANSI.SYS, and the requested change occurs. For example, to use the PROMPT command to clear your screen, enter the following:

```
C:\> PROMPT $e[2J
```

The [2J is the ANSI control sequence to clear the screen. The letter *J* must be uppercase. Each time you press the Enter key, the screen clears and the cursor moves to the upper-left corner. As you know, each time you press Enter, MS-DOS displays your prompt. In this case, your prompt clears the screen. To return to the default command prompt, enter this command:

```
C:\> PROMPT $p$g
```

One disadvantage of using the PROMPT command to send escape sequences to the screen is that you change your prompt each time you send an escape sequence. Fortunately, there is a way around this, which is discussed later in this chapter. Another disadvantage is that you must turn ECHO on in order for the characters from the PROMPT command to be interpreted by ANSI.SYS.

The other method for sending escape sequences to the screen is to use the ECHO command. Because you can't specify the escape character in an ECHO command at the command prompt, you can use ECHO to send an escape sequence only from a batch file.

The escape character cannot be displayed on screen. If you use the TYPE command to display a batch file containing an escape sequence, the sequence will be interpreted by ANSI.SYS rather than displayed on the screen. Like the bell character discussed earlier, the escape character is a control character that causes something to happen. In the case of the escape character, what happens is determined by the ANSI codes that follow the escape character.

For some control characters, such as the bell (^G), there is a convention for how the character should be displayed in a file. However, no such convention exists for the escape character. You can see the escape sequence in a text editor, but different editors display it differently. The steps required for inserting the escape character in a batch file also vary with the different text editors. This book will generally use the left-pointing arrow (←) to depict the escape character, because that's the symbol Edit uses.

To insert an escape character within Edit, you use the Ctrl-P sequence that was used previously to insert the bell character. Simply press the Ctrl key and the P key together. You can then press the Esc key to add the escape character to your text. It displays as a left-pointing arrow. To try this, open a new file named CLRSCRN.BAT in Edit by entering the following command:

```
C:\> EDIT CLRSCRN.BAT
```

Now type the word *ECHO* followed by a space. Next hold down the Ctrl key and press the P key. To insert the escape character, press the Esc key (usually located in the upper-left corner of your keyboard). Your screen should look like Figure 8-1.

FIGURE 8-1. *The screen representation of the escape character (the left-pointing arrow).*

Complete the command to clear the screen by entering *[2J* and pressing the Enter key. For the sequence to work, the *J* must be uppercase. Finally save the file (Alt-F,S) and exit the Edit program (Alt-F,X). When you enter the CLRSCRN command, your batch file clears the screen.

For those who prefer to use Edlin (or those who are using a version of MS-DOS earlier than 5 and must use Edlin), the key-combination used to insert the escape character is Ctrl-V. To create the same batch file in Edlin, start the program with the following command:

```
C:\> EDLIN CLRSCRN2.BAT
```

In your new file, you must first activate the Edlin insert mode by typing *I* and then pressing the Enter key. To begin the command, type the word *ECHO* and a single space. Next hold down the Ctrl key and press the V key. Your screen should now display this:

```
C:\> EDLIN CLRSCRN2.BAT
New file
*I
        ECHO ^V
```

The ^V represents the escape character. You now enter the ANSI control sequence for clearing the screen by typing *[2J.* (Remember to use an uppercase *J.*) Press Enter to move to the next line. On the next line, press Ctrl-C to exit Edlin's insert mode. Finally type *E* and press enter to exit Edlin and then save your file. Each time you use CRLSCRN2, the previous contents of your screen disappear and the cursor moves to the upper-left corner.

Of course, you can accomplish all of this by using the CLS command, but now you have an idea of how escape sequences are actually used to control the display. More importantly, you know how to enter the escape character in your batch files.

SETTING SCREEN COLORS

Let's start by using ANSI.SYS and the PROMPT command to set screen colors. The ANSI.SYS escape sequence to set your screen's color is as follows:

←[*color*m

The left-pointing arrow (←) is the ASCII escape character, the sequence ends with the letter *M*, and *color* is one of the color values defined in the following table:

color Value	Color
0	Default color (black and white)
1	Bold text attribute
2*	Low-intensity text attribute
3*	Italic text attribute
4	Underscore turned on for IBM monochrome; underscore color (blue) for VGA
5	Blinking text attribute
6*	Rapid-blinking text attribute
7	Reverse-video text attribute
8	Concealed text attribute
30	Black foreground
31	Red foreground
32	Green foreground
33	Yellow foreground
34	Blue foreground
35	Magenta foreground
36	Cyan foreground
37	White foreground
40	Black background

color Value	Color
41	Red background
42	Green background
43	Yellow background
44	Blue background
45	Magenta background
46	Cyan background
47	White background
48	Subscript
49*	Superscript

* Not operative on VGA monitors.

NOTE: *Not all values are supported in all versions of ANSI.SYS.*

For example, the following ANSI.SYS escape sequence sets the screen foreground color to red:

←[31m

Remember, the left arrow represents the escape character. The following sequence sets the screen background color to green:

←[42m

The following batch file, CYANBG.BAT, uses the PROMPT command's $e metacharacter (which represents escape) to set the screen background color to cyan:

```
PROMPT $e[46m
PROMPT [$p]
CLS
```

The $e metacharacter directs PROMPT to write the ASCII escape character. The first command sets the background color to cyan, and the second PROMPT command resets the command prompt to the current path (drive and directory), displayed within square brackets. The CLS command clears the screen display, which sets the entire screen's background color to cyan (rather than just the portion around the prompt).

In a similar manner, the next batch file, BLUEFG.BAT, uses the PROMPT command to set the screen's foreground color to blue:

```
PROMPT $e[34m
PROMPT [$p]
CLS
```

If you run this batch file, the ANSI.SYS device driver changes your screen's foreground to blue, leaving the screen background color unchanged.

Using SETCOLOR.BAT

As you can see, the CYANBG.BAT and BLUEFG.BAT batch files are almost identical—the only difference is the color value. You can create a batch file named SETCOLOR.BAT that sets the screen-color attributes based on the value of the %1 parameter. In this case, the batch file becomes the following:

```
IF "%1"=="" GOTO DONE
PROMPT $e[%1m
PROMPT [$p]
CLS
:DONE
```

To set your screen color, simply specify the color value as a batch-file parameter. For example, the following command line sets the screen's background color to green:

```
C:\> SETCOLOR 42
```

MS-DOS simply replaces %1 with the value 42, yielding this escape sequence:

```
←[42m
```

You can use this batch file to set either the foreground or background color. In fact, you can run it once to set the foreground, a second time to set the background, and a final time to set the text attribute. If you enter the following commands, you end up with blinking magenta text on a cyan background:

```
SETCOLOR 35
SETCOLOR 46
SETCOLOR 5
```

Use the SETCOLOR 0 command to reset the screen color to the default white foreground on black background.

Restoring the Prompt

The batch files discussed so far use the PROMPT command to generate the escape sequence that sets screen colors. In each case, the batch file ends with a PROMPT command that restores the prompt to the current drive and directory within square brackets, such as [C:\]. A better alternative is for the batch file to restore the prompt that was in effect when the batch file was started. The following batch file, SETCLR2.BAT, does just that:

```
IF "%1"=="" GOTO DONE
SET ORIGINAL_PROMPT=%PROMPT%
PROMPT $e[%1m
PROMPT %ORIGINAL_PROMPT%
SET ORIGINAL_PROMPT=
CLS
:DONE
```

The batch file begins by assigning the current prompt value to an environment variable called ORIGINAL_PROMPT. To make this assignment, the batch file uses the %PROMPT% named parameter. Each PROMPT command changes the value of %PROMPT%. Before the batch file ends, it restores the prompt by using the %ORIGINAL_ PROMPT% named parameter with the PROMPT command. By using named parameters in this way, batch files can minimize the number of side effects (unexpected changes that might occur as a result of the batch file's execution).

Of course, you could accomplish the same thing by using the ECHO command to change the screen color rather than the PROMPT command. Using that approach, the batch file would contain one line—the ECHO command with the replaceable parameter.

Using Text Attributes

You might be wondering when your batch files would use the bold, blinking, or reverse-video attributes available with ANSI.SYS. Consider an application that displays this message:

```
About to delete FILENAME.EXT
Press any key to continue . . .
```

Earlier in this book, you used the computer's built-in "bell" to get the user's attention before displaying a message with PAUSE. The following batch file, DELETE.BAT, uses the blinking text attribute to get the user's attention.

```
@ECHO OFF
IF "%1"=="" GOTO DONE
REM Set text attribute to blinking.
REM Must turn ECHO on for PROMPT command to
REM change the text attribute.
PROMPT $e[5m
ECHO ON
ECHO OFF
CLS
PROMPT [$p]
REM Displaying warning message
ECHO About to delete %1
PAUSE
DEL %1
PROMPT $e[0m
REM Restore default color. Again, turn ECHO on.
ECHO ON
ECHO OFF
PROMPT [$p]
:DONE
```

This batch file displays a blinking message as specified, but when it completes execution, it sets the screen color to its default setting. If you used ANSI.SYS to set your screen's color, that color is lost. To solve this problem, you must always set your screen colors with a batch file that records the values. The next batch file, SCRCOLOR.BAT, defines three named parameters—TEXTATTR, FOREGROUND, and BACKGROUND—as follows:

```
@ECHO OFF
:LOOP
IF "%1"=="" GOTO DONE
PROMPT $e[%1m
ECHO ON
ECHO OFF
PROMPT [$p]
CLS
@ECHO OFF
REM Set the named parameters TEXTATTR, FOREGROUND,
REM and BACKGROUND
IF "%1"=="0" SET TEXTATTR=0
IF "%1"=="1" SET TEXTATTR=1
IF "%1"=="2" SET TEXTATTR=2
IF "%1"=="3" SET TEXTATTR=3
IF "%1"=="4" SET TEXTATTR=4
IF "%1"=="5" SET TEXTATTR=5
IF "%1"=="6" SET TEXTATTR=6
IF "%1"=="7" SET TEXTATTR=7
IF "%1"=="8" SET TEXTATTR=8
IF "%1"=="30" SET FOREGROUND=30
```

```
IF "%1"=="31" SET FOREGROUND=31
IF "%1"=="32" SET FOREGROUND=32
IF "%1"=="33" SET FOREGROUND=33
IF "%1"=="34" SET FOREGROUND=34
IF "%1"=="35" SET FOREGROUND=35
IF "%1"=="36" SET FOREGROUND=36
IF "%1"=="37" SET FOREGROUND=37
IF "%1"=="40" SET BACKGROUND=40
IF "%1"=="41" SET BACKGROUND=41
IF "%1"=="42" SET BACKGROUND=42
IF "%1"=="43" SET BACKGROUND=43
IF "%1"=="44" SET BACKGROUND=44
IF "%1"=="45" SET BACKGROUND=45
IF "%1"=="46" SET BACKGROUND=46
IF "%1"=="47" SET BACKGROUND=47
IF "%1"=="48" SET BACKGROUND=48
IF "%1"=="49" SET BACKGROUND=49
SHIFT
GOTO LOOP
:DONE
```

As you can see, depending on the color value specified on the command line as the first parameter of SCRCOLOR.BAT, the batch file defines one of the three named parameters. The SHIFT command is used so you can enter all three values on a single command line.

You can then create a batch file that changes the screen attributes and tests to see whether one of the named parameters exists, and, if it does, restores the previous screen colors. Modifying DELETE.BAT to do this gives you the following:

```
@ECHO OFF
IF "%1"=="" GOTO DONE
REM Set text attribute to blinking.
REM Must turn ECHO on for PROMPT command to
REM change the text attribute.
SET ORIGINAL_PROMPT=%PROMPT%
PROMPT $e[5m
ECHO ON
ECHO OFF
CLS
PROMPT [$p]
REM Displaying warning message
ECHO About to delete %1
PAUSE
DEL %1
REM Restore default color. Again, turn ECHO on.
ECHO ON
IF NOT "%TEXTATTR%"=="" PROMPT $e[%TEXTATTR%m
IF NOT "%FOREGROUND%"=="" PROMPT $e[%FOREGROUND%m
```

(continued)

```
IF NOT "%BACKGROUND%"=="" PROMPT $e[%BACKGROUND%m
ECHO OFF
CLS
PROMPT %ORIGINAL_PROMPT%
SET ORIGINAL_PROMPT=
:DONE
```

Of course, for this batch file to work, you must have set the original screen attributes and colors using SCRCOLOR.BAT so that their values are stored as the environment entries. The only flaw with this batch file is that if you use Ctrl-C to stop the batch file (rather than continuing with the DEL operation), the screen attribute remains set to blinking. A better method is to use the ECHO command to set the screen attribute. This method also avoids having to modify the original prompt.

In many cases, you might want to draw attention to only a single word, which you can do by using the ECHO command rather than the PROMPT command. The following batch file, DELETE2.BAT, creates a warning message with the filename in blinking red on a white background. It then resets the screen attributes (assuming they were originally set with SCRCOLOR.BAT). In this batch file, several screen attributes are changed with a single ECHO command:

```
@ECHO OFF
IF "%1"=="" GOTO DONE
REM Display a warning message with the
REM filename set to blinking red on white.
CLS
ECHO About to delete ←[5m←[31m←[47m%1
REM Restore default color
ECHO ←[0m
IF NOT "%TEXTATTR%"=="" ECHO ←[%TEXTATTR%m
IF NOT "%FOREGROUND%"=="" ECHO ←[%FOREGROUND%m
IF NOT "%BACKGROUND%"=="" ECHO ←[%BACKGROUND%m
REM Provide the user the option to cancel or continue
ECHO Press Ctrl-C to cancel
PAUSE
REM Delete the file
DEL %1
:DONE
```

Because it is possible that no attributes were set before the batch file executed, the default attribute of white on black is reset before applying any attribute codes stored in %TEXTATTR%, %FOREGROUND%, or %BACKGROUND%. This technique turns off the attributes set within the batch file and then uses the environment entries to turn on those that were in effect when the batch file started. Again, this works only if SCRCOLOR.BAT was used to set the colors. As you can see in this example, a single ECHO or PROMPT command can set several attributes. The only flaw with this version is that each of the four ECHO commands used to restore the default color produces a blank line.

POSITIONING THE CURSOR

In addition to clearing your screen and setting the screen's foreground and background colors, you can use ANSI.SYS in your batch files to control the cursor's position on the screen. After you use an ANSI.SYS escape sequence to position the cursor, the next output appears on the screen at that position.

The following table lists the five ANSI.SYS cursor-positioning escape sequences:

Escape Sequence	Result
←[NumRowsA	Moves cursor up
←[NumRowsB	Moves cursor down
←[NumRowsC	Moves cursor right
←[NumRowsD	Moves cursor left
←[Row;ColH	Sets cursor at the Row,Col position

Most screens display 25 rows and 80 columns. The extreme upper-left corner of the screen is defined as 1,1—that is, row 1, column 1. The lower-right corner of the screen is defined as 25,80.

You can create this batch file, CURPOS.BAT, which uses the ECHO command and ANSI escape sequences to display messages at the: 1,1, 5,5, 10,10, and 20,20 screen positions:

```
CLS
ECHO ←[1;1HRow 1, Column 1
ECHO ←[5;5HRow 5, Column 5
ECHO ←[10;10HRow 10, Column 10
ECHO ←[20;20HRow 20, Column 20
```

The batch-file fragment on the following page illustrates how you might use the ANSI.SYS cursor-positioning escape sequences to display information about the CLS command. It displays the command name centered on the screen in bold and the information in a distinct color.

```
@ECHO OFF
CLS
ECHO ←[0M
ECHO ←[1M
ECHO ←[1;39HCLS
ECHO ←[34M
ECHO ←[3;10HCOMMAND TYPE:
ECHO ←[3;25HINTERNAL
ECHO ←[5;10HFUNCTION:
ECHO ←[5;25HErases the screen display, placing the cursor
ECHO ←[6;30Hat the upper-left, or home, position.
ECHO ←[8;10HEXAMPLE:
ECHO ←[8;25HCLS
```

In this case, the fragment first disables any currently set attributes to
avoid potential color conflicts. Then the batch file uses ANSI.SYS to
set the text attribute to bold and center the CLS command name. Next
the batch file selects the foreground color and displays the information.
As you can see, the batch file uses escape sequences of the following
form to position the text on the screen:

   ←[row;colH

The section titles (COMMAND TYPE:, FUNCTION:, and EXAM-
PLE:) are aligned in column 10. The entries for each section are aligned
in column 25. The second line of the FUNCTION entry is indented five
additional spaces (to column 30). You could insert escape sequences to
change the colors of the various parts of the display. For example, you
could make the titles white and the entry text blue. After the batch file
displays the CLS information, the batch file could reset the attributes as
shown in the previous example (assuming the attributes had been set
with SCRCOLOR.BAT).

REDEFINING KEYS

The ANSI.SYS device driver enhances both screen and keyboard
capabilities. You have just used ANSI.SYS to clear the screen, set
foreground and background colors, and position the cursor. To enhance your keyboard's capabilities, ANSI.SYS lets you redefine keys.

Each key on your keyboard is identified by a unique value. This value,
which is called a *scan code*, can be used with ANSI.SYS to assign a

text string to any key on the keyboard. Rather than typing a command or phrase, you can use this feature to assign the text to a particular key. In general, such assignments are made to the function keys rather than any of the standard keyboard characters.

Because F1 through F4 are used by MS-DOS for editing the command line and F1 through F9 and some function keys combined with Alt are used by DOSKEY, it is best to use a function key combined with Shift or Ctrl for your personal key assignments. The following scan codes are for the ten standard function keys combined with Shift and Ctrl:

Function Key	+Shift Scan Code	+Ctrl Scan Code
F1	84	94
F2	85	95
F3	86	96
F4	87	97
F5	88	98
F6	89	99
F7	90	100
F8	91	101
F9	92	102
F10	93	103

A table with scan codes for the standard keyboard characters is presented later in this chapter.

To assign a character string to one of the function keys, you use an ANSI.SYS escape sequence with the following form:

←[0;Scancode;"string"p

For example, to assign the VER command to the Shift-F7 key combination, the escape sequence is this:

←[0;90;"VER"p

Likewise, to assign the CLS command to the Shift-F10 key combination, the escape sequence is this:

←[0;93;"CLS"p

NOTE: *Because the scan codes in these examples specify special keys called* extended keys, *the first parameter of the escape sequence is a zero followed by a semicolon and the scan-code value. Extended keys include the function* *keys (F1 through F12), the arrow keys, the editing keys, and any of these keys combined with Shift, Ctrl, or Alt. You also have to include a zero as the first parameter of the escape sequence if you want to combine any other key with the Alt key. For scan codes that do not specify extended keys, omit the zero and its semicolon.*

The following batch file, DEFKEY.BAT, uses the ANSI.SYS keyboard-reassignment escape sequence to define a function key on the keyboard:

```
@ECHO OFF
IF "%1"=="" GOTO DONE
IF "%2"=="" GOTO DONE
ECHO ←[0;%1;"%2"p
:DONE
```

This batch file uses the %1 batch parameter to determine which function key (or key combination) to define and the %2 batch parameter to determine which value to assign to the key. For example, to assign the CLS command to the Shift-F10 key combination, your command line is this:

```
C:\> DEFKEY 93 CLS
```

As you can see, the batch file uses the values 93 and CLS to create this escape sequence:

```
ECHO ←[0;93;"CLS"p
```

You can assign a text string containing spaces to a key, as in the following command line:

```
C:\> DEFKEY 93 DIR *.* /P
```

To do this, simply change the DEFKEY.BAT batch file to use the %1 through %9 batch parameters, as follows:

```
IF "%1"=="" GOTO DONE
IF "%2"=="" GOTO DONE
ECHO ←[0;%1;"%2 %3 %4 %5 %6 %7 %8 %9"p
:DONE
```

After you create the DEFKEY.BAT batch file, you can run it from AUTOEXEC.BAT by using either the CALL or COMMAND /C command. Your keyboard definitions will then become active each time your system starts.

You've just had a glimpse of what can be done with keyboard reassignment and how it can be accomplished. The following table gives the scan codes for the extended keys and key combinations you might want to redefine:

Key/Key Combinations	Scan Code
Shift-Tab	15
Alt- q, w, e, r, t, y, u, i, o, p	16–25
Alt- a, s, d, f, g, h, j, k, l	30–38
Alt- z, x, c, v, b, n, m	44–50
F1–F10	59–68
Home	71
Up arrow	72
Page Up	73
Left arrow	75
Right arrow	77
End	79
Down arrow	80
Page Down	81
Insert	82
Delete	83
Shift-F1–Shift-F10	84–93
Ctrl-F1–Ctrl-F10	94–103
Alt-F1–Alt-F10	104–113

USING THE IBM EXTENDED CHARACTER SET

Your computer represents all digits, letters, and symbols using unique values ranging from 0 through 255. The first 128 values (from 0 through 127) represent the commonly used digits, letters, and punctuation characters. These values are known as the *ASCII character set*. The second 128 values (from 128 through 255) provide miscellaneous characters, including drawing symbols for IBM PC and compatible computers. These characters, which are known as the *IBM extended character set*, are shown in the table on the following page.

Char.	Value	Char.	Value	Char.	Value	Char.	Value
Ç	128	á	160	└	192	α	224
ü	129	í	161	┴	193	β	225
é	130	ó	162	┬	194	Γ	226
â	131	ú	163	├	195	π	227
ä	132	ñ	164	─	196	Σ	228
à	133	Ñ	165	┼	197	σ	229
å	134	ª	166	╞	198	µ	230
ç	135	º	167	╟	199	τ	231
ê	136	¿	168	╚	200	Φ	232
ë	137	⌐	169	╔	201	Θ	233
è	138	¬	170	╩	202	Ω	234
ï	139	½	171	╦	203	δ	235
î	140	¼	172	╠	204	∞	236
ì	141	¡	173	═	205	φ	237
Ä	142	«	174	╬	206	ε	238
Å	143	»	175	╧	207	∩	239
É	144	░	176	╨	208	≡	240
æ	145	▓	177	╤	209	±	241
Æ	146	█	178	╥	210	≥	242
ô	147	│	179	╙	211	≤	243
ö	148	┤	180	╘	212	⌠	244
ò	149	╡	181	╒	213	⌡	245
û	150	╢	182	╓	214	÷	246
ù	151	╖	183	╫	215	≈	247
ÿ	152	╕	184	╪	216	°	248
Ö	153	╣	185	┘	217	•	249
Ü	154	║	186	┌	218	·	250
¢	155	╗	187	█	219	√	251
£	156	╝	188	▄	220	η	252
¥	157	╜	189	▌	221	²	253
Pt	158	╛	190	▐	222	■	254
ƒ	159	┐	191	▀	223		255

As you become more skilled at creating batch files, you might want to enhance the screen displays your batch files produce by placing menus and other information in boxes. For example, you can create a batch file named BOXMENU.BAT that displays the following menu:

```
1 - Display directory listing

2 - Display MS-DOS version number

3 - Display disk volume label

4 - Quit
```

Enter your choice (1, 2, 3, or 4):

The batch file uses the IBM extended character values 179, 191, 192, 196, 217, and 218 to draw the box, as follows:

```
┌ 218          196               191 ┐


│ 179                           179 │
                                  .

└ 192          196               217 ┘
```

This batch file can be created using Edit or, if necessary, Edlin. To begin using Edit, start a new file named BOXMENU.BAT with the following command:

```
C:\> EDIT BOXMENU.BAT
```

Then enter the @ECHO OFF and CLS commands, as well as the label :LOOP.

Next, on a new line, type *ECHO*, but don't press Enter. Hold down the Alt key and type *218* on the numeric keypad at the far right of your keyboard. (If you are working in Edlin, you can use the same technique to insert the character—Alt plus the ASCII code.) When you release the Alt key, your screen displays the upper-left corner of the box, as follows:

```
@ECHO OFF
CLS
:LOOP
ECHO ┌
```

Next hold down the Alt key and type *196* on the numeric keypad. When you release the Alt key, MS-DOS displays one horizontal line character that extends the top (horizontal) part of the box, as follows:

```
@ECHO OFF
CLS
:LOOP
ECHO ┌─
```

Type 34 more horizontal line characters:

```
@ECHO OFF
CLS
:LOOP
ECHO ┌─────────────────────────────────
```

Complete the top of the box with the upper-right corner by holding down the Alt key and typing *191*:

```
@ECHO OFF
CLS
:LOOP
ECHO ┌──────────────────────────────────┐
```

Using the IBM extended character value 179 for the vertical bar character, complete the next seven lines as follows:

```
@ECHO OFF
CLS
:LOOP
ECHO ┌──────────────────────────────────┐
ECHO │ 1 - Display directory listing    │
ECHO │                                  │
ECHO │ 2 - Display MS-DOS version number │
ECHO │                                  │
ECHO │ 3 - Display disk volume label    │
ECHO │                                  │
ECHO │ 4 - Quit                         │
```

The bottom of the box is much like the top, except that you must use the IBM extended character values 192 and 217 for the lower-left and lower-right corners of the box.

Now that you have created your menu display, you need to provide the commands that perform the actions. In MS-DOS versions 6 or later, the easiest way to do this is by using the CHOICE command. To complete the batch file, enter the following:

```
REM Evaluate menu choices
CHOICE Enter your choice (1, 2, 3, or 4): /c1234 /n
IF ERRORLEVEL 1 IF NOT ERRORLEVEL 2 GOTO DO_DIR
IF ERRORLEVEL 2 IF NOT ERRORLEVEL 3 GOTO DO_VER
IF ERRORLEVEL 3 IF NOT ERRORLEVEL 4 GOTO DO_VOL
IF ERRORLEVEL 4 IF NOT ERRORLEVEL 5 GOTO EXIT
GOTO LOOP

REM Perform action based on menu choice
:DO_DIR
DIR
PAUSE
GOTO LOOP

:DO_VER
VER
PAUSE
GOTO LOOP
```

```
:DO_VOL
VOL
PAUSE
GOTO LOOP

:EXIT
```

Your completed batch file contains these commands:

```
ECHO
ECHO  ┌─────────────────────────────────────┐
ECHO  │ 1 - Display directory listing       │
ECHO  │                                     │
ECHO  │ 2 - Display MS-DOS version number   │
ECHO  │                                     │
ECHO  │ 3 - Display disk volume label       │
ECHO  │                                     │
ECHO  │ 4 - Quit                            │
ECHO  └─────────────────────────────────────┘
```

```
REM Evaluate menu choices
CHOICE Enter your choice (1, 2, 3, or 4): /c1234 /n
IF ERRORLEVEL 1 IF NOT ERRORLEVEL 2 GOTO DO_DIR
IF ERRORLEVEL 2 IF NOT ERRORLEVEL 3 GOTO DO_VER
IF ERRORLEVEL 3 IF NOT ERRORLEVEL 4 GOTO DO_VOL
IF ERRORLEVEL 4 IF NOT ERRORLEVEL 5 GOTO EXIT
GOTO LOOP

REM Perform action based on menu choice
:DO_DIR
DIR
GOTO LOOP

:DO_VER
VER
GOTO LOOP

:DO_VOL
VOL
GOTO LOOP

:EXIT
```

The IBM extended character set gives you greatly expanded screen-presentation capabilities. For example, by adding a few more ECHO commands to the previous batch file, you can create a menu that looks like the one on the following page.

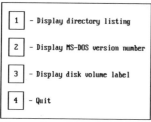

Enter your choice (1, 2, 3, or 4):

You can further enhance the appearance of your menu by using the
IBM extended character value 219 to add a shadow box like this:

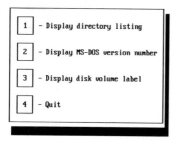

Enter your choice (1, 2, 3, or 4):

As you can see, the use of the shadow box gives the menu a profes-
sional flair. By now you have put together a powerful collection of
batch-processing tools. Show off your skills by using the examples
in this chapter to develop professional-quality screen displays.

CHAPTER 9

Enhancing Batch Files with DEBUG Programs

CREATING PROGRAMS WITH DEBUG

The standard batch-file commands provide you with a powerful set of basic tools, but what happens if you want to create a batch file that requires a tool you don't have? The answer is to create your own tools with DEBUG.

DEBUG is a programmer's utility designed to help programmers find errors, or bugs, in their programs. It can also be used to create small programs using *assembly language*. Assembly language is a set of commands that can be executed directly by your computer without first being processed by MS-DOS.

Very few of the 80 million or so MS-DOS users are programmers. And even fewer know how to program in assembly language. Fortunately, you don't have to know how to program to create the utilities in this chapter. As with most DEBUG programs used in batch files, someone else has developed the actual instructions. You simply need to enter them in the proper order. Each example explains all the steps and, if you follow along carefully, you will find DEBUG very easy to use.

Most people who regularly develop batch files have a collection of utilities created with DEBUG, but very few of those people create the utilities themselves. Most of their DEBUG programs are copied from magazine articles and other published sources. Don't worry about copyrights for these types of programs—they're published so that you can use them in your own batch files. In this chapter, you will create the following programs:

Program	Purpose
SCRPRINT	Prints the screen from within your batch file.
REBOOT	Causes your system to reboot from within your batch file.

(continued)

(continued)

Program	Purpose
GETYORN	Provides an alternative to the CHOICE command for obtaining Yes or No responses from the user.
F1TOF10	Lets you use the F1 through F10 keys as input to your batch file.
GETARROW	Lets you use the Up arrow and Down arrow within menus and other batch files.
BELL	Sounds the system beep.
SCANCODE	Determines what key was pressed on the keyboard.
WRITE	Provides an alternative to the ECHO command.

In addition, DEBUG is used in Chapter 11 to create a series of utilities for determining the current time and date.

There are two ways to create programs using DEBUG, both of which are covered in this chapter. The first method is to start DEBUG and enter the program line by line. We start with this method so that you can get a feel for how DEBUG actually works. With the second method, you create files, called DEBUG scripts, that contain the necessary instructions. Rather than typing the instructions in DEBUG, you enter the instructions in a text file and then redirect the file to the DEBUG command. The second method is the way DEBUG programs are commonly presented in magazines and other sources. If you work through all of the examples in this chapter, you will know how to create any DEBUG programs you find in other sources, regardless of which method the authors of the programs use.

There is one other bit of knowledge you need before you can work with the DEBUG program: hexadecimal notation. You don't really need to know too much about the topic, but you should understand that DEBUG programs count with a different numbering system than you are used to. Instead of ten digits, hexadecimal notation uses sixteen: 0, 1, 2, 3, 4, 5, 6, 7, 8, 9, A, B, C, D, E, and F. This means that the value 10H (the H indicates a hexadecimal number) is equal to 16 because you count from 0 through 15 (or F) in the rightmost column and then represent the value 16 as 1 in the next column to the left. (This works the same as counting from 0 through 9 in the rightmost column and then representing the value 10 as 1 in the next column to the left in decimal notation.) Thus in hexadecimal, A1H is equal to 161 (1 in the rightmost column and then A x 16—or 10 x 16—in the next column to the left).

If you find this confusing, don't worry. If you carefully follow the instructions, you won't have any trouble using DEBUG.

To begin, let's create a program named SCRPRINT.COM that prints the current contents of your screen display. Assume that your batch file displays important data on the screen and you want to ensure that the user saves this information. After displaying the data, your batch file can run SCRPRINT to print the screen's contents.

When you run DEBUG, you can specify on the command line the name of the file that DEBUG is to create, like this:

```
C:\> DEBUG FILENAME.EXT
```

Creating a New File

To begin, run DEBUG with the SCRPRINT.COM filename as its parameter:

```
C:\> DEBUG SCRPRINT.COM
```

DEBUG responds with this message:

```
C:\> DEBUG SCRPRINT.COM
File not found
```

-

The message *File not found* tells you that SCRPRINT.COM does not already exist on disk. The hyphen (-) is DEBUG's prompt.

Entering the Print Screen Program

Type the command *A 100* and press the Enter key:

```
C:\> DEBUG SCRPRINT.COM
File not found

-A 100
5AFF:0100
```

The A 100 command tells DEBUG that you want to enter program commands at a special location designated by the hexadecimal address 100. Each time MS-DOS runs a program, MS-DOS begins execution at this location—so that's where we will place our instructions. All the programs you will create using DEBUG will start with A 100.

DEBUG responds to the A 100 command by displaying a line number: for example, 5AFF:0100. The rightmost number, 0100, is the address you specified in the preceding line, 100. (In the instructions that follow, the line numbers shown in the programs are in hexadecimal. For example, if you are counting by twos, the first eight line numbers are: 0100, 0102, 0104, 0106, 0108, 010A, 010C, and 010E.) The number displayed to the left of 0100 on your screen might be different from the number shown here because the leftmost number depends on where MS-DOS starts DEBUG in memory, which version of MS-DOS you are running, and which programs you have installed.

To enter your first command, type the *INT 5* command and press Enter:

```
C:\> DEBUG SCRPRINT.COM
File not found

-A 100
5AFF:0100 INT 5
5AFF:0102
```

The INT 5 command directs your computer to print its screen contents.

It's as easy as that! Next you must include two more instructions that tell MS-DOS to end the program. First type *MOV AH, 4C* and press Enter. Second type *INT 21* and press Enter. Your program is complete.

Saving the File

You must now tell DEBUG to save the program's contents on disk. To start the save process for the program, press Enter. DEBUG displays its hyphen prompt, like this:

```
C:\> DEBUG SCRPRINT.COM
File not found

-A 100
5AFF:0100 INT 5
5AFF:0102 MOV AH, 4C
5AFF:0104 INT 21
5AFF:0106
-
```

Next type the *R CX* command, and DEBUG responds like this:

```
-R CX
CX 0000
:
```

CX is a built-in register, or storage location, that is used by DEBUG to hold the program's size. Before DEBUG can write the program on disk, you must tell DEBUG how large the program is. You determine the size by taking the address value from the last line number in the program and subtracting the address value from the first line number:

```
C:\> DEBUG SCRPRINT.COM
File not found

-A 100
5AFF:0100 INT 5  ◄──────────── First program line number
5AFF:0102 MOV AH, 4C
5AFF:0104 INT 21
5AFF:0106  ◄──────────── Last program line number
-R CX
CX 0000
:
```

In this case, 0106 minus 0100 equals 6, so your program is 6 bytes long. Type *6* at the colon prompt to place this value in the CX register. When you press Enter, DEBUG displays its command prompt, as follows:

```
C:\> DEBUG SCRPRINT.COM
File not found

-A 100
5AFF:0100 INT 5
5AFF:0102 MOV AH, 4C
5AFF:0104 INT 21
5AFF:0106
-R CX
CX 0000
:6
-
```

Now to save the file on disk, you issue the DEBUG write command, W:

```
C:\> DEBUG SCRPRINT.COM
File not found

-A 100
5AFF:0100 INT 5
5AFF:0102 MOV AH, 4C
5AFF:0104 INT 21
5AFF:0106
-R CX
CX 0000
:6
-W
Writing 00006 bytes
-
```

Quitting DEBUG

After DEBUG saves the file on disk, use the DEBUG quit command,
Q, to return to the command prompt:

```
C:\> DEBUG SCRPRINT.COM
File not found

-A 100
5AFF:0100 INT 5
5AFF:0102 MOV AH, 4C
5AFF:0104 INT 21
5AFF:0106
-R CX
CX 0000
:6
-W
Writing 00006 bytes
-Q

C:\>
```

Using Your New Program

If you request a directory listing of the SCRPRINT.COM file, MS-DOS
displays the following:

```
C:\> DIR SCRPRINT.COM
 Volume in drive C is DOS 6 DISK
 Volume Serial Number is 3A2F-18E9
 Directory of  C:\BATCH

SCRPRINT COM         6 04-11-93  12:11p
        1 File(s)          6 bytes
                    21155840 bytes free
```

As you can see, the size of the file is 6 bytes.

You can now run the SCRPRINT program from the command prompt
to print the current screen contents.

AUTOMATING A WARM BOOT

If your batch file makes changes to your system configuration, you will
need to reboot your system for the changes to take effect. You can do

this by pressing the Ctrl-Alt-Del key combination, but the whole point of creating a batch file is to automate the process. The following steps create the DEBUG program, REBOOT.COM, which reboots your system as though you had pressed Ctrl-Alt-Del:

```
C:\> DEBUG REBOOT.COM
File not found

-A 100
584B:0100 MOV AX, 40
584B:0103 MOV DS, AX
584B:0105 MOV AX, 1234
584B:0108 MOV [72], AX
584B:010B JMP FFFF:0
584B:0110
-R CX
CX 0000
:10
-W
Writing 00010 bytes
-Q

C:\>
```

REBOOT.COM places the value 1234 in memory and then uses the JMP command to branch to the bootstrap program that boots your computer when you turn it on. The bootstrap program examines the 4072H memory location to see if it contains the value 1234. If it does, the program performs a warm reboot. Otherwise, it performs a cold boot just as if you had turned your machine off and then on again. The following program includes comments that explain REBOOT.COM's processing:

```
:0100 MOV AX, 40    ; First portion of the hexadecimal address
:0103 MOV DS, AX
:0105 MOV AX, 1234  ; Prepare the value to be inserted
:0108 MOV [72], AX  ; Move value into the memory address
:010B JMP FFFF:0    ; Jump to bootstrap program
```

Because the first four digits of the addresses will probably be different on your system, they are not included in this listing. You can start entering the program from any memory address. Just be sure to start with A 100 as your first instruction. You can enter comments in your program if you precede them with a semicolon (;).

Now when you run REBOOT.COM from the command prompt, your computer reboots.

Controlling a RAM Drive with REBOOT

Let's consider an application where you might need a batch file to reboot your computer. Assume that, like many people, you use a portion of memory as a RAM drive to simulate a fast disk drive. After you create a RAM drive, you can access it using a single drive letter and a colon—exactly as you would access a hard drive or floppy drive. Because the RAM drive resides in your computer's memory, it does not have the mechanical constraints of a hard drive or floppy drive. As a result, the RAM drive gives you a faster storage location for your files. However, the RAM drive is temporary; when you turn off your computer, the contents of your RAM drive are lost.

Depending on your version of MS-DOS, you use either RAM-DRIVE.SYS or VDISK.SYS to create a RAM drive. With MS-DOS versions 3.2 and later, you create the RAM drive by using the CONFIG.SYS DEVICE= entry to load the RAMDRIVE.SYS device driver into memory. For example, the following entry creates a 64-KB RAM drive (the default size), which consumes 10 percent of your conventional memory:

```
DEVICE=RAMDRIVE.SYS
```

To create a 256-KB RAM drive, which consumes 40 percent of your conventional memory, use this entry:

```
DEVICE=RAMDRIVE.SYS 256
```

NOTE: *You must reboot your system for CONFIG.SYS changes to take effect.*

If you install a RAM drive for your daily computer operations, you might have to remove the RAM drive to run application programs that require large amounts of memory. Each time you need to remove the RAM drive from memory, you must edit your CONFIG.SYS file by removing the DEVICE=RAMDRIVE.SYS entry and then reboot your computer. If you want to reinstall the RAM drive, you must again edit CONFIG.SYS and again reboot.

NOTE: *If you are using MS-DOS version 6 or later, you can take advantage of multiple configurations. The following batch file will not work with multiple configuration CONFIG.SYS files unless the RAMDRIVE entry is in a concluding [common] block.*

Rather than continually repeating this edit–reboot cycle, you can create the following batch file, RAMDRIVE.BAT, which performs this task for you:

```
@ECHO OFF
IF "%1"=="INSTALL" GOTO INSTALL_DISK
IF "%1"=="UNLOAD" GOTO UNLOAD_DISK
GOTO DONE
:INSTALL_DISK
REM Install the RAM drive by adding a DEVICE=RAMDRIVE.SYS
REM entry to CONFIG.SYS. Use %2 to determine the
REM size of the RAM drive. After CONFIG.SYS is
REM updated, reboot.
IF NOT EXIST \CONFIG.SYS GOTO ADD_ENTRY
REM
REM Remove all lines in CONFIG.SYS containing RAMDRIVE.
REM
TYPE \CONFIG.SYS | FIND /V /I "RAMDRIVE" > \CONFIG.NEW
DEL \CONFIG.SYS
REM
REM Append the RAMDRIVE entry to CONFIG.SYS.
REM
:ADD_ENTRY
ECHO DEVICE=RAMDRIVE.SYS %2 >> \CONFIG.NEW
REN \CONFIG.NEW CONFIG.SYS
REBOOT
GOTO DONE
:UNLOAD_DISK
REM Remove the RAM drive by removing the RAMDRIVE entry
REM from CONFIG.SYS and rebooting.
IF NOT EXIST \CONFIG.SYS GOTO DONE
REM
REM Remove all lines in CONFIG.SYS containing RAMDRIVE.
REM
TYPE \CONFIG.SYS | FIND /V /I "RAMDRIVE" > \CONFIG.NEW
DEL \CONFIG.SYS
REN \CONFIG.NEW CONFIG.SYS
REBOOT
:DONE
```

To install a 128-KB RAM drive, you run the batch file with a command line like this:

```
C:\> RAMDRIVE INSTALL 128
```

In this case, the batch file installs a RAM drive capable of storing 128 KB. To unload the RAM drive, you run the batch file with this command line:

```
C:\> RAMDRIVE UNLOAD
```

In both cases, the batch file edits CONFIG.SYS and reboots your computer so that the changes take effect.

This batch file requires that the REBOOT program created in the last section be available (either in the current directory or on the search path). Similarly, the ECHO command following the ADD_ENTRY label assumes that the RAMDRIVE.SYS file can be found in the root directory. If that is not the case, you must provide the appropriate path in addition to the filename—for example, C:\DOS\RAMDRIVE.SYS.

In the section of the batch file starting with the ADD_ENTRY label, the GOTO DONE command following the REBOOT command is intended never to be executed, because the system should reboot. However, if REBOOT does not exist or cannot be found, GOTO DONE ensures that the remainder of the batch file is not executed.

GETTING A YES OR NO RESPONSE

If you are using MS-DOS version 6 or later, you can use the CHOICE command in your batch files to get a Yes or No response from the user. If you are not using MS-DOS 6 or later, you can create the following program, GETYORN.COM, to get a Yes or No response:

```
C:\> DEBUG GETYORN.COM
File not found

-A 100
5B10:0100 MOV AH, 08 ; Prepare character service
5B10:0102 INT 21     ; Call the service
5B10:0104 CMP AL, 59 ; Did user press Y?
5B10:0106 JZ 010E    ; If so, jump to line 010E
5B10:0108 CMP AL, 4E ; Did user press N?
5B10:010A JZ 010E    ; If so, jump to line 010E
5B10:010C JMP 0100   ; Loop to get valid character
5B10:010E MOV AH, 4C ; Prepare program termination service
5B10:0110 INT 21     ; Call the service
5B10:0112
-R CX
CX 0000
:12
-W
Writing 00012 bytes
-Q

C:\>
```

As you can see, the program is slightly more complex than those in the previous two examples. However, if you type it exactly as it appears, you will have no problems. You do not need to include the comments, but if you do, be sure to use the semicolon (;).

When the Y or N key is pressed, GETYORN.COM returns the key's scan code as an exit-status value (89 for Y and 78 for N). A batch file can then use the following IF commands to process the Yes or No response:

```
IF ERRORLEVEL 89 GOTO YES
IF ERRORLEVEL 78 GOTO NO
```

Notice that the batch file should first test for the higher exit-status value (89). The IF ERRORLEVEL command returns a value of true when the specified value is greater than or equal to the exit-status value. If the batch file first tests for an exit-status value of 78, MS-DOS always executes the corresponding commands because both keys return values greater than or equal to 78.

This program uses the MS-DOS character service to obtain the value of the key that was pressed. An MS-DOS service is a mechanism that enables programs to access MS-DOS directly for performing tasks. The service that retrieves a character's value is prepared with the statement MOV AH, 08 and initiated with the next statement (INT 21). The value returned is placed in register AL. The statement CMP AL, 59 compares that value to the hexadecimal value 59 (89 in decimal). If the two values are equal, the key pressed was a Y, and the program jumps to line 010E. If the two values are not equal, the program checks whether the key was an N. If it was, the program jumps to line 010E. If it wasn't, the program returns to line 0100 to get another key. Line 010E prepares the MS-DOS character service that will move the key's scan-code value to ERRORLEVEL and end the program. Again, the INT 21 statement actually initiates the action. Note that this program checks for Y and N, not y and n.

Selectively Copying Files with GETYORN

After you create GETYORN.COM, you can put it to use immediately in a batch file like COPYYN.BAT, which is shown on the following page.

This batch file uses the FOR and COPY commands, to allow you to selectively copy files to a disk in drive A:

```
@ECHO OFF
REM Create a temporary batch file named COPYIT.BAT that
REM prompts the user to copy a file to the A drive.
REM If the user presses Y, the batch file copies
REM the file. If the user presses N, the batch file
REM does not copy the file.
REM Use ECHO and MS-DOS redirection to create the
REM batch file.
ECHO ECHO Do you want to copy %%1? > COPYIT.BAT
ECHO GETYORN >> COPYIT.BAT
ECHO IF ERRORLEVEL 89 COPY %%1 A: >> COPYIT.BAT

REM Now that COPYIT.BAT exists on disk, use it within
REM the FOR loop. First, remind the user to insert a disk.
ECHO Make sure you have a disk in drive A:
PAUSE

FOR %%C IN (%1) DO CALL COPYIT %%C

REM The COPYIT.BAT batch file is no longer needed.
DEL COPYIT.BAT
```

Actually, COPYYN.BAT creates a temporary batch file that it uses to
copy the files one at a time. When the temporary batch file, COPY-
IT.BAT, is no longer needed, COPYYN.BAT deletes it.

Let's examine the three lines that create the batch file:

```
ECHO ECHO Do you want to copy %%1? > COPYIT.BAT
ECHO GETYORN >> COPYIT.BAT
ECHO IF ERRORLEVEL 89 COPY %%1 A: >> COPYIT.BAT
```

The batch file uses the MS-DOS output redirection operator (>) to
create the batch file named COPYIT.BAT. The next two commands
use the MS-DOS append redirection operator (>>) to add commands to
the batch file. Notice the use of the double percent signs in %%1. As
you will recall, each time MS-DOS detects %1 in a batch file, MS-DOS
substitutes the value of the first batch-file parameter. In this case, however, we don't want MS-DOS to substitute a parameter; instead, we
want MS-DOS to write the characters %1 to the COPYIT.BAT batch
file. Using the double percent signs achieves this result and allows
COPYIT.BAT to support batch-file parameters.

The primary processing in COPYYN.BAT occurs in the FOR loop,
which passes each filename to the COPYIT.BAT batch file. Each time
the FOR loop calls COPYIT.BAT, the batch file asks whether the

specified filename should be copied. The batch file then uses the
GETYORN.COM program, which we just created, to determine the
response. If Y is pressed (a Yes response), the batch file copies the file.
If N is pressed (a No response), COPYIT.BAT completes execution,
skipping the COPY command, and the FOR loop repeats.

You can run COPYYN.BAT with the following command line:

```
C:\> COPYYN *.*
```

The batch file then allows you to selectively copy any file in the current
directory to a disk in drive A.

SCANNING FOR FUNCTION KEYS

In a manner similar to the GETYORN.COM program, the following
program, F1TOF10.COM, returns the keyboard scan-code values 59
through 68 corresponding to the F1 through F10 keys. (In the following
listing, the first four digits of the address have been omitted.)

```
C:\> DEBUG F1TOF10.COM
File not found

 -A 100
:0100 MOV AH, 08 ; Prepare character service
:0102 INT 21     ; Call the service
:0104 CMP AL, 0  ; Is first portion 0 (Is if function key)
:0106 JNZ 0100   ; If it wasn't 0, return to 0100 and try again
:0108 MOV AH, 08 ; Next, prepare service to get next portion
:010A INT 21     ; Call the service
:010C CMP AL, 3B ; Compare scan code to 3B (F1)
:010E JL 0100    ; If less than 3B, jump to 0100 and try again
:0110 CMP AL, 44 ; Compare scan code to 44 (F10)
:0112 JG 0100    ; If greater than 44, jump to 0100 and try again
:0114 MOV AH, 4C ; Prepare program termination service
:0116 INT 21     ; Call the service
:0118
 -R CX
CX 0000
: 18
 - W
Writing 00018 bytes
 - Q

C:\>
```

Whereas the GETYORN program compared the character and jumped
to the end if the user pressed Y or N, the F1TOF10 program checks that

the value is within the proper range for a function key. If it's not, the program returns for another character. The scan-code value returned for a function key consists of two segments: a zero followed by the number identifying the key pressed. The statement on line 0104 checks that the first value is zero. If it isn't, the program immediately returns to get another character. Only if the first value is zero is the second value even tested. The next lines cause values below 3B (59 in decimal) or above 44 (68 in decimal) to be rejected, and the program tries the next character.

You can use the F1T0F10.COM program in a batch file such as DOSMENU.BAT, which displays this menu:

```
F1 - Display directory listing
F2 - Display MS-DOS version number
F3 - Display disk volume label
F4 - Quit
```

If the F1 key is pressed, the batch file displays a directory listing. If the F2 key is pressed, the batch file displays the current MS-DOS version number. If the F3 key is pressed, the batch file displays the volume label. The batch file continues this processing until you press F4 to quit. Here are the commands for DOSMENU.BAT:

```
@ECHO OFF
CLS
:LOOP
ECHO F1 - Display directory listing
ECHO F2 - Display MS-DOS version number
ECHO F3 - Display disk volume label
ECHO F4 - Quit
REM Get user response
:GET_KEY
F1TOF10
IF ERRORLEVEL 63 GOTO GET_KEY
IF ERRORLEVEL 62 GOTO DONE
IF ERRORLEVEL 61 IF NOT ERRORLEVEL 62 VOL
IF ERRORLEVEL 60 IF NOT ERRORLEVEL 61 VER
IF ERRORLEVEL 59 IF NOT ERRORLEVEL 60 DIR
GOTO LOOP
:DONE
```

The batch file first displays the menu and then runs the F1TOF10 program to get a function-key response. F1TOF10 requires the user to press a function key between F1 and F10. This batch file further restricts the keys that can be pressed. If a function key from F5 through F10 is pressed, the batch file loops back to get a valid key. If the F4 key (scan code 62) is pressed, the batch file ends. Notice the use of the nested IF commands to test for a specific exit-status value. By using two IF commands in this manner, the batch file can test whether the exit-status value is precisely 61, 60, or 59, instead of testing whether the value is greater than or equal to one of these values.

ACCEPTING UP ARROW, DOWN ARROW, OR ENTER

The last program we'll look at in this section, GETARROW.COM, waits for the user to press the Up arrow key, the Down arrow key, or the Enter key. The program returns an exit-status value of 72 for Up arrow and a value of 80 for Down arrow. If the Enter key is pressed, the batch file returns an exit-status value of 13. The program does not exit until one of these three keys is pressed. Here's how to create the GETARROW.COM program:

```
C:\> DEBUG GETARROW.COM
File not found

-A 100
:0100 MOV AH, 8
:0102 INT 21
:0104 CMP AL, D
:0106 JZ 11A
:0108 CMP AL, 0
:010A JNZ 100
:010C MOV AH, 8
:010E INT 21
:0110 CMP AL, 48
:0112 JZ 11A
:0114 CMP AL, 50
:0116 JZ 11A
:0118 JMP 100
:011A MOV AH, 4C
:011C INT 21
:011E
-R CX
CX 0000
:1E
-W
Writing 0001E bytes
-Q

C:\>
```

This program relies upon the MS-DOS character service to obtain the last key pressed. As with GETYORN.COM, this program checks for matches to certain scan codes. If the scan code of the key pressed matches any of the three desired ones, the program ends and returns the scan code in ERRORLEVEL. If the scan code doesn't match, the program returns to get another character (line 0118). The first comparison is for the Enter key (with a scan code of 13 in decimal or D in hexadecimal) on line 0104 (CMP AL, D). If the key was the Enter key, the program jumps to the end (line 0106). Because the arrow keys have a two-part scan code (like the function keys in the previous program), the next test checks for a value of zero as the first portion (line 0108). If the value is not zero, the program jumps back to line 0100 (line 010A). The program then goes on to check whether the second portion of the scan code identifies the Up arrow (a scan-code value of 72 or 48H; line 0110) or the Down arrow (a scan-code value of 80 or 50H; line 0114). If it identifies either, the program jumps to the end (lines 0112 and 0116). Otherwise, the program returns to line 0100.

NOTE: *This is the first program whose size in bytes has been an obvious hexadecimal number (1E). In reality, the bytes have always been reported in hexadecimal. When you wrote the REBOOT.COM program, it reported that it was writing 10 bytes. If you look at a directory listing of the file, you will see that it actually requires 16 bytes of storage. The value 10 in hexadecimal is equal to the value 16 in decimal. The GETARROW.COM program is actually 31 bytes in a directory listing.*

You can use this program in a batch file like ARROW.BAT, which displays a menu similar to that of the previous batch file:

```
Display directory
Display MS-DOS version
Display volume label
Quit
```

In this case, the batch file uses the ANSI.SYS device driver to highlight the current menu selection. The current selection changes as the Up or Down arrow key is pressed. When the Enter key is pressed, the batch file executes the command that corresponds to the current selection:

```
@ECHO OFF
SET CURRENT=DIR
:LOOP
CLS
IF %CURRENT%==DIR ECHO ←[1mDisplay directory
IF NOT %CURRENT%==DIR ECHO ←[0mDisplay directory
```

```
IF %CURRENT%==VER ECHO ←[1mDisplay MS-DOS version
IF NOT %CURRENT%==VER ECHO ←[0mDisplay MS-DOS version
IF %CURRENT%==VOL ECHO ←[1mDisplay volume label
IF NOT %CURRENT%==VOL ECHO ←[0mDisplay volume label
IF %CURRENT%==QUIT ECHO [1mQuit
IF NOT %CURRENT%==QUIT ECHO ←[0mQuit
GETARROW
IF ERRORLEVEL 80 GOTO DOWN_ARROW
IF ERRORLEVEL 72 GOTO UP_ARROW
IF %CURRENT%==DIR DIR
IF %CURRENT%=VER VER
IF %CURRENT%==VOL VOL
IF %CURRENT%==QUIT GOTO DONE
PAUSE
GOTO LOOP

:UP_ARROW
IF NOT %CURRENT%==DIR GOTO UP_VER
SET CURRENT=QUIT
GOTO LOOP
:UP_VER
IF NOT %CURRENT%==VER GOTO UP_VOL
SET CURRENT=DIR
GOTO LOOP
:UP_VOL
IF NOT %CURRENT%==VOL GOTO UP_QUIT
SET CURRENT=VER
GOTO LOOP
:UP_QUIT
SET CURRENT=VOL
GOTO LOOP

:DOWN_ARROW
IF NOT %CURRENT%==DIR GOTO DOWN_VER
SET CURRENT=VER
GOTO LOOP
:DOWN_VER
IF NOT %CURRENT%==VER GOTO DOWN_VOL
SET CURRENT=VOL
GOTO LOOP
:DOWN_VOL
IF NOT %CURRENT%==VOL GOTO DOWN_QUIT
SET CURRENT=QUIT
GOTO LOOP
:DOWN_QUIT
SET CURRENT=DIR
GOTO LOOP

:DONE
ECHO ←[0m
SET CURRENT=
```

The menu-manipulation capabilities demonstrated in this batch file are normally restricted to programs written in languages such as Pascal or C. This batch file uses the %CURRENT% named parameter to keep track of the current selection. When the batch file begins execution, it uses the SET command to assign the value DIR to the named parameter. (If you look at the menu displayed by ARROW.BAT, you'll see that DIR is the first selection.) Next the batch file uses the IF command to determine the current selection and the ANSI.SYS escape sequence ←[1m to display the current selection in bold. The batch file uses the escape sequence ←[0m to display all the other options with the normal attribute. See Chapter 8 for more information about escape sequences.

Next the batch file uses the GETARROW.COM program, which we just created, to get the Up arrow, Down arrow, or Enter key. If the Enter key is pressed, the batch file uses the %CURRENT% named parameter to determine which command to execute. If either the Up arrow or Down arrow key is pressed, the batch file determines the new current selection and redisplays the menu.

When the Quit option is selected, the batch file resets the attribute to normal and removes the %CURRENT% named parameter from the MS-DOS environment.

Admittedly, this batch file's menu options are quite basic; however, ARROW.BAT illustrates the amount of programming you can perform using MS-DOS batch files.

NOTE: *As you can see, ARROW.BAT repeatedly invokes GETARROW.COM to determine which key has been pressed. By storing GETARROW.COM on a RAM drive and then invoking the command from the RAM drive, you can make the batch file execute much faster.*

CREATING PROGRAMS USING DEBUG SCRIPT FILES

So far, you have created programs interactively by typing instructions from within DEBUG. Many people (and computer magazine examples) create programs using DEBUG script files. In general, a DEBUG script file is nothing more than a file that contains the keystrokes you would normally type to create the program interactively within DEBUG. As a rule, DEBUG script files have the SCR extension.

You can create DEBUG script files using Edit or Edlin. For example, the following DEBUG script file, BELL.SCR, contains the instructions necessary to create a program named BELL.COM that sounds the computer's built-in speaker:

```
N BELL.COM
A 100
MOV DL, 7
MOV AH, 2
INT 21
MOV AH, 4C
INT 21

R CX
A
W
Q
```

After you create a text file named BELL.SCR that contains these commands, redirect its contents to the DEBUG command, like this:

```
C:\> DEBUG < BELL.SCR
```

DEBUG, in turn, creates the BELL.COM program, which a batch file can invoke when it needs to get attention. Each line from the script executes a command within DEBUG. The actual steps are displayed on your screen as BELL.COM is created. You can now use BELL.COM in your batch files as follows:

```
@ECHO OFF
BELL
BELL
ECHO Do you want to delete %1?
REM Remainder of the batch-file commands here.
```

AN ALTERNATIVE TO CHOICE

If you are using MS-DOS version 6 or later, the CHOICE command makes it easy to prompt for a keyboard response and then determine which key was pressed. If you are not using MS-DOS version 6 or later, you can use the DEBUG script file SCANCODE.SCR, shown on the following page, to create the SCANCODE.COM program, which returns the scan code of the key pressed.

```
N SCANCODE.COM
A 100
XOR AH, AH
INT 16
CMP AH, 0
JE 100
MOV AL, AH
MOV AH, 4C
INT 21

R CX
10
W
Q
```

Create the script file, and then redirect its contents to DEBUG, like this:

```
C:\> DEBUG < SCANCODE.SCR
```

You can then incorporate SCANCODE.COM into any batch file, and the program will return an exit-status value corresponding to the key pressed. Figure 9-1 shows the possible scan-code values.

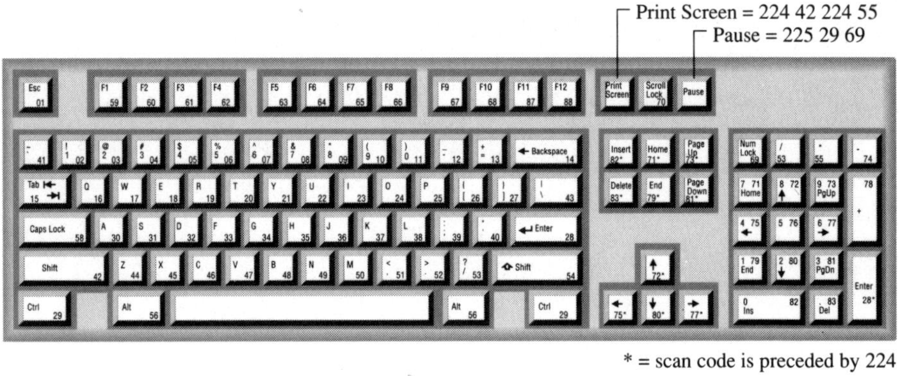

FIGURE 9-1. *The keyboard, showing all possible scan codes.*

REPLACING ECHO WITH WRITE

As the complexity of your batch files increases, there will be times when you'll want your batch files to write messages to the screen without moving the cursor to the next line (as the ECHO command does). The DEBUG script file on the following page, WRITE.SCR, creates a program named WRITE.COM that displays a line of output without a carriage-return and linefeed character.

```
N WRITE.COM
A 100
MOV BX, 80
INC BX
CMP BYTE [BX], D
JNE 103
MOV BYTE [BX], 24
MOV AH, 9
MOV DX, 82
CMP DX, BX
JG 117
INT 21
MOV AH, 4C
INT 21

R CX
1B
W
Q
```

As before, use DEBUG as follows to create the program file:

```
C:\> DEBUG < WRITE.SCR
```

You can then use WRITE.COM and SCANCODE.COM in a batch file
to display a prompt and wait for a key to be pressed, as follows:

```
WRITE Enter choice:
SCANCODE
```

When the batch file executes, your screen displays the prompt without
moving the cursor to the next line, as shown here:

```
Enter choice:_
```

In Chapter 10 you will use the WRITE.COM program again, this time
to help build batch files "on-the-fly."

CHAPTER 10

Building a Batch-File Library

SETTING SCREEN COLORS

So far we have looked at several simple batch files that you might use on a daily basis. In this chapter we add six more general-purpose batch procedures to your collection. As you work with these batch files, feel free to modify them to meet your needs.

The first batch file, COLORS.BAT, lets you use your keyboard's arrow keys to cycle through the background screen colors supported by the ANSI.SYS device driver. (For this batch file to successfully execute, your CONFIG.SYS file must have loaded the ANSI.SYS device driver into memory.) Each time you press the Up arrow or Down arrow key, the batch file changes the screen color. When you press the Enter key, the selected color remains active for the remainder of your session.

```
@ECHO OFF
REM Allow the user to cycle through the background
REM screen colors that are available, until the user
REM presses Enter to select a color.
SET CURRENT=BLACK
:LOOP
IF %CURRENT%==BLACK ECHO ←[40m
IF %CURRENT%==RED ECHO ←[41m
IF %CURRENT%==GREEN ECHO ←[42m
IF %CURRENT%==YELLOW ECHO ←[43m
IF %CURRENT%==BLUE ECHO ←[44m
IF %CURRENT%==MAGENTA ECHO ←[45m
IF %CURRENT%==CYAN ECHO ←[46m
IF %CURRENT%==WHITE ECHO ←[47m
CLS
ECHO Press Enter to select the current color
ECHO Use Up arrow and Down arrow to change colors
GETARROW
```

```
IF ERRORLEVEL 80 GOTO DOWN_ARROW
IF ERRORLEVEL 72 GOTO UP_ARROW
IF ERRORLEVEL 13 GOTO DONE

:DOWN_ARROW
IF NOT %CURRENT%==BLACK GOTO DN_RED
SET CURRENT=RED
GOTO LOOP
:DN_RED
IF NOT %CURRENT%==RED GOTO DN_GREEN
SET CURRENT=GREEN
GOTO LOOP
:DN_GREEN
IF NOT %CURRENT%==GREEN GOTO DN_YELLOW
SET CURRENT=YELLOW
GOTO LOOP
:DN_YELLOW
IF NOT %CURRENT%==YELLOW GOTO DN_BLUE
SET CURRENT=BLUE
GOTO LOOP
:DN_BLUE
IF NOT %CURRENT%==BLUE GOTO DN_MAGENTA
SET CURRENT=MAGENTA
GOTO LOOP
:DN_MAGENTA
IF NOT %CURRENT%==MAGENTA GOTO DN_CYAN
SET CURRENT=CYAN
GOTO LOOP
:DN_CYAN
IF NOT %CURRENT%==CYAN GOTO DN_WHITE
SET CURRENT=WHITE
GOTO LOOP
:DN_WHITE
SET CURRENT=BLACK
GOTO LOOP

:UP_ARROW
IF NOT %CURRENT%==BLACK GOTO UP_RED
SET CURRENT=WHITE
GOTO LOOP
:UP_RED
IF NOT %CURRENT%==RED GOTO UP_GREEN
SET CURRENT=BLACK
GOTO LOOP
:UP_GREEN
IF NOT %CURRENT%==GREEN GOTO UP_YELLOW
SET CURRENT=RED
GOTO LOOP
```

(continued)

```
:UP_YELLOW
IF NOT %CURRENT%==YELLOW GOTO UP_BLUE
SET CURRENT=GREEN
GOTO LOOP
:UP_BLUE
IF NOT %CURRENT%==BLUE GOTO UP_MAGENTA
SET CURRENT=YELLOW
GOTO LOOP
:UP_MAGENTA
IF NOT %CURRENT%==MAGENTA GOTO UP_CYAN
SET CURRENT=BLUE
GOTO LOOP
:UP_CYAN
IF NOT %CURRENT%==CYAN GOTO UP_WHITE
SET CURRENT=MAGENTA
GOTO LOOP
:UP_WHITE
SET CURRENT=CYAN
GOTO LOOP

:DONE
```

Although long, the COLORS.BAT batch file is simple. The batch file uses the %CURRENT% named parameter to track the current background color. Based on the value of %CURRENT%, the batch file echos the corresponding ANSI.SYS escape sequence to the screen display. The batch file uses the GETARROW.COM program, which we created using DEBUG in Chapter 9. The batch file starts by setting the value of %CURRENT% to black. Next it uses the value of %CURRENT% to set the background color. You are then presented with a choice of pressing the Up arrow, Down arrow, or Enter key.

If you press an arrow key, the batch file determines whether it is an Up arrow or a Down arrow. If it is an Up arrow, the batch file jumps to the UP_ARROW label and begins looking for the current screen color. When the batch file locates the current color, the name of the next color in sequence (white, cyan, magenta, blue, yellow, green, red, or black) is assigned to %CURRENT%. The batch file then returns to the LOOP label at the top of the batch file and resets the background color based on the new value of %CURRENT%.

Notice that the IF statements are organized in the reverse order by color and are designed to jump to the next test if the current color does not match. The Down arrow is handled in a similar fashion by the group of statements that start with the DOWN_ARROW label.When you press Enter, the batch file completes execution.

PREVENTING HARD-DISK FORMATTING

Many hard disks have fallen victim to errant FORMAT commands issued by novice users. To prevent accidental formatting, many people remove the FORMAT.COM file from their hard disks. Removing the FORMAT.COM file does eliminate the possibility of accidentally formatting the hard disk, but it also removes a necessary MS-DOS command. Most people back up their work on floppy disks and will probably need the FORMAT command to format floppy disks.

Here's an alternate solution. Rename the FORMAT command as FMAT.COM, and then create a batch file named FORMAT.BAT that contains the following commands:

```
@ECHO OFF
ECHO To prevent inadvertent formatting of the hard
ECHO disk, this batch file lets you format only
ECHO floppy disks in drive A or B. Specify the disk
ECHO drive to use in your command line.
ECHO Example: FORMAT A:
CHOICE Do you want to continue
IF ERRORLEVEL 1 IF NOT ERRORLEVEL 2 GOTO CONTINUE_FORMAT
IF ERRORLEVEL 2 GOTO DONE

:CONTINUE_FORMAT
IF "%1"=="" GOTO NO_PARAMS
IF "%1"=="A:" GOTO VALID_DRIVE
IF "%1"=="a:" GOTO VALID_DRIVE
IF "%1"=="B:" GOTO VALID_DRIVE
IF "%1"=="b:" GOTO VALID_DRIVE
GOTO INVALID_DRIVE

:NO_PARAMS
ECHO You must specify the disk drive to format
ECHO in your command line.
GOTO DONE

:VALID_DRIVE
FMAT %1 %2 %3 %4 %5 %6 %7 %8 %9
GOTO DONE

:INVALID_DRIVE
ECHO This batch file formats only disks in
ECHO drive A or B. The batch file considers
ECHO the disk drive %1 invalid.

:DONE
```

This batch file lets you format only floppy disks in either drive A or drive B. When you run this batch file, MS-DOS displays this message:

```
To prevent inadvertent formatting of the hard
disk, this batch file lets you format only
floppy disks in drive A or B. Specify the disk
drive to use in your command line.
Example: FORMAT A:
Do you want to continue [Y,N]?
```

If you press Y, the batch file first tests to make sure you specified a drive. If you didn't, this error message is displayed:

```
You must specify the disk drive to format
in your command line.
```

The batch file then stops. If a drive was specified, the batch file tests to see whether it is a valid drive. (It is necessary to test for both uppercase and lowercase to make the batch file user-friendly.) If the %1 parameter contains a valid drive letter, the batch file jumps to the VALID_DRIVE label and uses FMAT.COM to format the disk. Otherwise, the batch file goes to the INVALID_DRIVE label and displays an error message.

NOTE: *In some cases, the FORMAT command line requires additional parameters, such as /S or /4. By using the %2 through %9 parameters, the batch file supports these additional command-line parameters.*

GETTING CHARACTER-STRING INPUT

In Chapter 9 you used DEBUG to create programs that allow the user to press the Y or N key to indicate a Yes or No response, to press a specific function key, and to press the Up arrow and Down arrow keys. In some cases, however, your batch files might need to get several characters, such as a filename or password, instead of a single key.

The following batch file, GETPASS.BAT, prompts you to enter a password and then compares this password with the predefined password MANAGEMENT. If the two passwords are identical, the batch file continues processing; otherwise, the batch file displays an error message and stops processing. Admittedly, you probably won't need to get a password for many batch-file applications, but GETPASS.BAT does demonstrate how to obtain user input from within your batch files. For example, you could use the same technique to pass a filename from the user to another command.

```
@ECHO OFF
IF NOT EXIST PASSWORD.SET GOTO NO_FILE
ECHO Enter your password, press F6, and then
ECHO press Enter.
COPY CON PASSWORD.DAT > NUL
COPY PASSWORD.SET+PASSWORD.DAT PASSWORD.BAT > NUL
CALL PASSWORD
IF NOT "%PASSWORD%"=="MANAGEMENT" GOTO BAD_PASSWORD
ECHO Valid password; ready to process payroll.
REM Insert protected commands here
GOTO DONE

:NO_FILE
ECHO This batch file requires the file PASSWORD.SET,
ECHO which contains SET PASSWORD=^Z
GOTO DONE

:BAD_PASSWORD
ECHO Invalid password

:DONE
SET PASSWORD=
DEL PASSWORD.BAT > NUL
DEL PASSWORD.DAT > NUL
```

The batch file relies on a file named PASSWORD.SET, which you can create from the command prompt. The batch file first tests for the existence of this file and if it is not available, stops processing. To create PASSWORD.SET, issue the following command:

```
C:\> COPY CON PASSWORD.SET
```

Next type *SET PASSWORD=*, but do not press Enter. Instead, immediately following the equal sign, press the F6 function key and then press Enter. When you do this, MS-DOS creates the file PASSWORD.SET. The steps in creating PASSWORD.SET result in the following screen display:

```
C:\> COPY CON PASSWORD.SET
SET PASSWORD=^Z
    1 File(s) copied

C:\>
```

When you run the GETPASS.BAT batch file, it prompts you to enter a password, as shown here:

```
Enter your password, press F6, and then
press Enter.
```

The batch file copies what you type into a file named PASS-WORD.DAT. This processing is accomplished by this command:

```
COPY CON PASSWORD.DAT > NUL
```

This command line directs MS-DOS to copy input from the keyboard to the PASSWORD.DAT file until you press F6 to signify the end of the file. The greater than symbol (>) redirects this message to the NUL device:

```
1 File(s) copied
```

The message does not appear on your screen.

Next this command directs MS-DOS to create the batch file PASS-WORD.BAT by appending the contents of PASSWORD.DAT to the contents of the PASSWORD.SET file:

```
COPY PASSWORD.SET+PASSWORD.DAT PASSWORD.BAT > NUL
```

Assuming that you typed the password *MANAGEMENT*, the file PASS-WORD.BAT now contains the following:

```
SET PASSWORD=MANAGEMENT
```

GETPASS.BAT then runs the newly created PASSWORD.BAT batch file, which creates the %PASSWORD% named parameter in the MS-DOS environment. The GETPASS.BAT batch file (our original program) can then compare the password with *MANAGEMENT* using the IF command. If the passwords differ, the batch file displays an error message and stops processing. If the passwords are the same, the batch file executes its protected commands. Notice that, before completing execution, the batch file removes the %PASSWORD% named parameter from the environment, as well as the PASSWORD.BAT and PASS-WORD.DAT files. To protect the password that appears in the batch file, use the ATTRIB command to hide GETPASS.BAT.

Using WRITE.COM to Improve PASSWORD.BAT

GETPASS.BAT currently requires that you create the PASS-WORD.SET file, which contains the following entry:

```
SET PASSWORD=
```

Ideally the batch file should not require the existence of such a file. Instead, the batch file should create the file itself, deleting the file when it is no longer needed. Because the file exists only when the batch file is in use, it does not consume unnecessary disk space. To create the PASS-WORD.BAT file without having to first create PASSWORD.SET, you can change the GETPASS batch file to use WRITE.COM, which you created in Chapter 9, as shown here:

```
@ECHO OFF
WRITE SET PASSWORD=> PASSWORD.BAT
ECHO Enter your password, press F6, and then
ECHO press Enter.
COPY PASSWORD.BAT+CON PASSWORD.BAT > NUL
CALL PASSWORD
IF NOT "%PASSWORD%"=="MANAGEMENT" GOTO BAD_PASSWORD
ECHO Valid password; ready to process payroll.
REM Insert protected commands here
GOTO DONE

:BAD_PASSWORD
ECHO Invalid password

:DONE
SET PASSWORD=
DEL PASSWORD.BAT
```

The WRITE.COM program writes the text *SET PASSWORD=* to the PASSWORD.BAT file. The COPY command then appends the characters that you type to the file. For example, if you type *MANAGEMENT* and press F6, the file contains the command SET PASSWORD= MANAGEMENT. When the CALL command invokes the batch file, MS-DOS creates the required environment entry.

SIMPLIFYING YOUR SYSTEM-BACKUP OPERATIONS

MS-DOS versions 6 and later provide the Microsoft Backup program, which is a very powerful menu-driven backup utility. You can start the program by typing the MSBACKUP command at the command prompt. If you are not using MS-DOS versions 6 or later, you can create batch files to help you automate your daily and monthly backups. These batch files use the BACKUP command available in versions 5 and earlier. The next batch file we discuss, FILEBU.BAT, helps you perform disk-backup operations. When you run this batch file, MS-DOS displays this:

```
F1 - Monthly Backup
F2 - Daily/Incremental Backup
F3 - Specific Files Backup
F4 - Quit
```

If you press the F1 key, the batch file performs a full backup—a backup of every file on your disk. Depending on the number of files you have, a monthly backup can be quite time-consuming.

If you press the F2 key, the batch file performs an incremental backup, backing up only those files that have been created or modified since the last full backup. An incremental backup can be much faster than a full backup, but you must keep all your incremental backup disks from one full backup to another to ensure that you have a copy of every file.

If you press the F3 key, the batch file prompts you to specify which files to back up, as well as the target disk drive. For example, to back up all the files in the DOS directory to the floppy disk in drive A, you enter this:

```
C:\DOS A:
```

Next press the F6 key, and then press Enter. The batch file goes to work, backing up only the files you specify.

If you press the F4 key, the batch file stops processing.

For ease of understanding, we'll examine this batch file as four distinct batch files: FILEBU.BAT, MONTHLY.BAT, DAILY.BAT, and SPECIFIC.BAT. The FILEBU.BAT file contains these commands:

```
@ECHO OFF
REM Allow the user to perform a monthly, daily, or
REM specific file backup.
CLS
REM Loop until the user presses the F4 key to quit.
:LOOP
ECHO F1 - Monthly Backup
ECHO F2 - Daily/Incremental Backup
ECHO F3 - Specific Files Backup
ECHO F4 - Quit
REM Get user response.
:GET_KEY
F1TOF10
REM If user presses a key other than F1 through F4, get
REM another key.
IF ERRORLEVEL 63 GOTO GET_KEY
IF ERRORLEVEL 62 GOTO DONE
IF ERRORLEVEL 61 IF NOT ERRORLEVEL 62 CALL SPECIFIC
IF ERRORLEVEL 60 IF NOT ERRORLEVEL 61 CALL DAILY
IF ERRORLEVEL 59 IF NOT ERRORLEVEL 60 CALL MONTHLY
GOTO LOOP
:DONE
```

As you can see, this batch file displays the main menu and then uses the F1TOF10.COM program, which we created in Chapter 9, to get a function key from the user. Depending on the function key pressed, the batch file calls either MONTHLY.BAT for a full backup, DAILY.BAT for an incremental backup, or SPECIFIC.BAT for backup of specific files. The batch file continues to loop, repeating this process until you press the F4 key to quit.

The MONTHLY.BAT batch file performs a full backup. When you select this option, MS-DOS displays the following:

```
The monthly backup copies all the files on
your hard disk to a floppy disk.

Depending on the number of files on your disk,
the monthly backup can be quite time-consuming.
Do you wish to continue [Y,N]?
```

This message simply explains the monthly-backup procedure and lets you continue or cancel the operation. If you respond by pressing Y, the BACKUP command backs up the entire disk to floppy disks in drive A. MONTHLY.BAT contains the following:

```
REM Perform a complete backup of the hard disk.
ECHO The monthly backup copies all the files on
ECHO your hard disk to a floppy disk.
ECHO.
ECHO Depending on the number of files on your disk,
ECHO the monthly backup can be quite time-consuming.
CHOICE Do you wish to continue
IF ERRORLEVEL 1 IF NOT ERRORLEVEL 2 GOTO BACKUP
IF ERRORLEVEL 2 GOTO RETURN
:BACKUP
ECHO Be sure that you label each disk with the
ECHO current date, the words MONTHLY BACKUP, and
ECHO your initials.
BACKUP C:\*.* A: /S
:RETURN
CLS
```

NOTE: *This batch file uses the CHOICE command. If you are using MS-DOS version 5 or earlier, you will need to use an ECHO command, the GETYORN.COM program (created in Chapter 9), and the appropriate values in the IF statements.*

The DAILY.BAT batch file shown on the following page is very similar to the MONTHLY.BAT batch file.

```
REM Perform a backup of each file on the disk changed
REM or created since the last full backup.

ECHO The daily backup copies all the files on
ECHO your hard disk that have been changed or created
ECHO since the last complete backup to floppy disk.
ECHO.
CHOICE Do you wish to continue
IF ERRORLEVEL 1 IF NOT ERRORLEVEL 2 GOTO BACKUP
IF ERRORLEVEL 2 GOTO RETURN
:BACKUP
ECHO Be sure that you label each disk with the
ECHO current date, the words DAILY BACKUP, and
ECHO your initials. Use the disk from the previous
ECHO daily backup until the floppy fills.
BACKUP C:\*.* A: /S /A /M
:RETURN
CLS
```

As you can see, if the user responds by pressing Y to continue the batch
file, the BACKUP command executes an incremental backup of all the
changed files on the hard disk.

Of the four backup batch files, SPECIFIC.BAT is the most interesting.
This batch file lets you specify the names of the files to be backed up.
The following listing shows how SPECIFIC.BAT depends on a file
named BACKUP.FMT that you can create at the command prompt:

```
REM Back up one or more user-specified files to disk.
REM Prompt the user to enter the filename to back up.
REM Copy the names to the BACKUP.DAT file. Using the
REM BACKUP.FMT file, create a BACKUP command in the
REM BACKIT.BAT batch file.
IF NOT EXIST BACKUP.FMT GOTO NO_FORMAT
ECHO The specific-file option allows you to back up
ECHO one or more files.
CHOICE Do you want to continue
IF ERRORLEVEL 1 IF NOT ERRORLEVEL 2 GOTO BACKUP
IF ERRORLEVEL 2 GOTO RETURN
NO_FORMAT:
ECHO The specific-file backup requires the file
ECHO BACKUP.FMT, which contains BACKUP ^Z
PAUSE
GOTO RETURN
:BACKUP
ECHO Type the drive, path, and name of the file to back up,
ECHO identify the target drive, press the F6 key,
ECHO and then press Enter.
ECHO Example: *.DAT A: ^Z [Enter]
COPY CON BACKUP.DAT > NUL
COPY BACKUP.FMT+BACKUP.DAT BACKIT.BAT
```

```
CALL BACKIT
DEL BACKUP.DAT
DEL BACKIT.BAT
:RETURN
CLS
```

You begin the specific-file backup by using the COPY CON BACK-UP.FMT command:

```
C:\> COPY CON BACKUP.FMT
```

Type *BACKUP* followed by a space, and press F6 to mark the end of the file:

```
C:\> COPY CON BACKUP.FMT
BACKUP ^Z
```

When you press Enter, MS-DOS creates the file, as follows:

```
C:\> COPY CON BACKUP.FMT
BACKUP ^Z
    1 File(s) copied

C:\>
```

If BACKUP.FMT does not exist, the batch file displays an error message and returns to the main menu. If BACKUP.FMT does exist, when you press Y to continue, the batch file prompts you to type the filename to back up as well as the target disk drive:

```
Type the drive, path, and name of the file to back up,
identify the target drive, press the F6 key,
and then press Enter.
Example: *.DAT A: ^Z [Enter]
```

The batch file stores the information you type in the BACKUP.DAT file. This command redirects its output to the NUL device:

```
COPY CON BACKUP.DAT > NUL
```

It thus suppresses the display of the message *1 File(s) copied.*

Next this command appends the contents of the BACKUP.DAT file (which contains the filename you want to back up) to the BACK-UP.FMT file (which contains the BACKUP command):

```
COPY BACKUP.FMT+BACKUP.DAT BACKIT.BAT
```

The resulting file is a batch file named BACKIT.BAT, which the batch file runs next. Assuming that you type *C:\DOS* and then type *A:*, the BACKIT.BAT file contains this command:

```
BACKUP C:\DOS A:
```

This command backs up only the desired directory. When the
BACKUP command completes execution, the batch file deletes the
BACKUP.DAT and BACKIT.BAT files, cleaning up after itself.

As demonstrated earlier in this chapter, you can use the WRITE com-
mand, which was created in Chapter 9, to eliminate the need for the
BACKUP.FMT file by adding the BACKUP command to BACK-
IT.BAT from within the batch file as shown here:

```
WRITE BACKUP > BACKIT.BAT
ECHO Type the drive, path, and name of the file to back up,
ECHO press the F6 key, and then press Enter.
ECHO Example: *.DAT A: ^Z [Enter]
COPY BACKIT.BAT+CON BACKIT.BAT > NUL
CALL BACKIT
DEL BACKIT.BAT
```

This collection of batch files shows you how easy it is to develop powerful utilities. To enhance these batch files, you might consider using
the ANSI.SYS device driver to add color, as described in Chapter 8. If
you are using MS-DOS version 3.3 or later, you might also want to add
the /L switch to the BACKUP command, which directs BACKUP to
create a log file. Also, you might consider adding exit-status checks
using IF ERRORLEVEL to display error messages if BACKUP fails.

BUILDING BATCH FILES "ON-THE-FLY"

Sometimes your batch file will need to invoke a second batch file to perform some simple processing. For example, the following batch file,
ASK_DEL.BAT, invokes a batch file named ASK_EM.BAT, which
determines whether you want to delete specific files:

```
@ECHO OFF
FOR %%I IN (%1) DO CALL ASK_EM %%I
```

The ASK_EM.BAT batch file contains the following commands:

```
CHOICE Do you want to delete %1
IF ERRORLEVEL 1 IF NOT ERRORLEVEL 2 DEL %1
```

With this batch file, you can specify a group of files using wildcards,
and then the batch file prompts you before deleting each one. This is a
batch-file version of the /P switch on the DEL command. In this case, a
fairly simple task requires two batch files. As discussed in Chapter 9,
small batch files can consume large amounts of disk space. Rather than

storing these two batch files on disk at all times, you can have the
ASK_DEL.BAT batch file create ASK_EM.BAT as it is needed:

```
@ECHO OFF
ECHO CHOICE Do you want to delete %%1 > ASK_EM.BAT
ECHO IF ERRORLEVEL 1 IF NOT ERRORLEVEL 2 DEL %%1 >> ASK_EM.BAT

FOR %%I IN (%1) DO CALL ASK_EM %%I
DEL ASK_EM.BAT
```

The ASK_DEL.BAT file creates the two-line ASK_EM.BAT batch file
by redirecting the output of the two ECHO commands. After the FOR
command completes execution, the batch file deletes ASK_EM.BAT.
In this way, the ASK_EM.BAT batch file exists on your disk only as it
is needed. By building batch files like this one on-the-fly, you conserve
disk space and simplify your batch processing because you have to manage fewer files.

A QUICK CALENDAR

Throughout this book you have used the ECHO command to display
messages on the screen to the user. Using only ECHO, you can create a
wide variety of batch files. For example, the following batch file,
JUNE_94.BAT, uses ECHO to create a batch file that displays the cal-
endar for the month of June, 1994:

```
@ECHO OFF
ECHO  S  M  T  W  T  F  S
ECHO           1  2  3  4
ECHO  5  6  7  8  9 10 11
ECHO 12 13 14 15 16 17 18
ECHO 19 20 21 22 23 24 25
ECHO 26 27 28 29 30 31
```

When you execute this batch file, your screen displays the following:

```
C:\> DEC_93
  S  M  T  W  T  F  S
           1  2  3  4
  5  6  7  8  9 10 11
 12 13 14 15 16 17 18
 19 20 21 22 23 24 25
 26 27 28 29 30
```

Chapter 11 will show you how to use different date and time commands
to make your batch files even more powerful.

Making Your Batch Files Aware of the Date and Time

FINDING THE DAY OF THE WEEK

Now that you have seen all the MS-DOS batch-file commands, learned how to create programs using DEBUG, and created several complex batch files, let's take a look at a few fun batch files that you might want to run from your AUTOEXEC.BAT file. All the batch files in this section use simple programs that you can create with DEBUG.

The first batch file, GREETING.BAT, uses the WEEKDAY.COM program to determine the current day of the week. The batch file then displays a message appropriate for that day. Here is the batch file:

```
@ECHO OFF
REM Determine the day of the week using the program
REM WEEKDAY.COM. The program returns a status value
REM that you can check by using the IF ERRORLEVEL
REM command. Sunday has the value 0, Monday has the
REM value 1, and so on. Saturday has the value 6.
REM After the batch file determines the day, it
REM displays an appropriate message.
WEEKDAY
IF ERRORLEVEL 0 IF NOT ERRORLEVEL 1 GOTO SUNDAY
IF ERRORLEVEL 1 IF NOT ERRORLEVEL 2 GOTO MONDAY
IF ERRORLEVEL 2 IF NOT ERRORLEVEL 3 GOTO TUESDAY
IF ERRORLEVEL 3 IF NOT ERRORLEVEL 4 GOTO WEDNESDAY
IF ERRORLEVEL 4 IF NOT ERRORLEVEL 5 GOTO THURSDAY
IF ERRORLEVEL 5 IF NOT ERRORLEVEL 6 GOTO FRIDAY
IF ERRORLEVEL 6 GOTO SATURDAY

:SUNDAY
ECHO It's Sunday - Relax and watch football.
GOTO DONE
```

```
:MONDAY
ECHO It's Monday - Get ready for a new week.
GOTO DONE

:TUESDAY
ECHO It's Tuesday - Week is just beginning.
GOTO DONE

:WEDNESDAY
ECHO It's Wednesday - Hump day!
GOTO DONE

:THURSDAY
ECHO It's Thursday - Almost there!
GOTO DONE

:FRIDAY
ECHO It's finally Friday - Happy Hour!
GOTO DONE

:SATURDAY
ECHO It's Saturday - You should be in bed.

:DONE
```

If you have an appointment or meeting that you don't want to forget, you can modify the ECHO statement for the day of the appointment or meeting or for the day before it to act as a reminder.

GREETING.BAT relies on a program named WEEKDAY.COM that uses the MS-DOS Get Date service to determine the day of the week. The program returns an exit-status value of 0 for Sunday, 1 for Monday, and so on. You can create WEEKDAY.COM using a DEBUG script named WEEKDAY.SCR, as follows:

```
N WEEKDAY.COM
A 100
MOV AH, 2A
INT 21
MOV AH, 4C
INT 21

R CX
8
W
Q
```

You store these lines in a text file called WEEKDAY.SCR and then re-direct the file's contents to DEBUG, as shown here:

```
C:\> DEBUG < WEEKDAY.SCR
```

FINDING THE MONTH

In a similar manner, the next batch file, SCHEDULE.BAT, uses a program named GETMONTH.COM to determine the current month. After the batch file determines the month, it branches to commands specific to that month and displays a list of dates and meetings:

```
@ECHO OFF
REM Determine the current month using the program
REM GETMONTH.COM. The program returns an exit-status value
REM from 1 through 12 that represents the current month.
REM (January is 1; December is 12.) After the month
REM is determined, branch to the specified month and
REM display important dates for the month.

GETMONTH
IF ERRORLEVEL 1 IF NOT ERRORLEVEL 2 GOTO JANUARY
IF ERRORLEVEL 2 IF NOT ERRORLEVEL 3 GOTO FEBRUARY
IF ERRORLEVEL 3 IF NOT ERRORLEVEL 4 GOTO MARCH
IF ERRORLEVEL 4 IF NOT ERRORLEVEL 5 GOTO APRIL
IF ERRORLEVEL 5 IF NOT ERRORLEVEL 6 GOTO MAY
IF ERRORLEVEL 6 IF NOT ERRORLEVEL 7 GOTO JUNE
IF ERRORLEVEL 7 IF NOT ERRORLEVEL 8 GOTO JULY
IF ERRORLEVEL 8 IF NOT ERRORLEVEL 9 GOTO AUGUST
IF ERRORLEVEL 9 IF NOT ERRORLEVEL 10 GOTO SEPTEMBER
IF ERRORLEVEL 10 IF NOT ERRORLEVEL 11 GOTO OCTOBER
IF ERRORLEVEL 11 IF NOT ERRORLEVEL 12 GOTO NOVEMBER
IF ERRORLEVEL 12 GOTO DECEMBER

:JANUARY
ECHO January  1 - New Year's Day
ECHO January 15 - Martin Luther King's Birthday
GOTO DONE

:FEBRUARY
ECHO February 12 - Lincoln's Birthday
ECHO February 14 - Valentine's Day
ECHO February 22 - Washington's Birthday
GOTO DONE

:MARCH
ECHO March 17 - St. Patrick's Day
GOTO DONE

:APRIL
ECHO April 1 - April Fools' Day
GOTO DONE
```

```
:MAY
ECHO May 1 - May Day
ECHO Last Monday in May - Memorial Day
GOTO DONE

:JUNE
GOTO DONE

:JULY
ECHO July 4 - Independence Day
GOTO DONE

:AUGUST
GOTO DONE

:SEPTEMBER
ECHO First Monday in September - Labor Day
GOTO DONE

:OCTOBER
ECHO Second Monday in October - Columbus Day
ECHO October 31 - Halloween
GOTO DONE

:NOVEMBER
ECHO November 11 - Veterans' Day
ECHO Fourth Thursday - Thanksgiving Day
GOTO DONE

:DECEMBER
ECHO Hanukkah begins
ECHO December 25 - Christmas

:DONE
```

In this example, the batch file lists several major holidays. Using the ECHO command, you can easily add birthdays, anniversaries, or other important dates.

You create the GETMONTH.COM program using the following GETMONTH.SCR script:

```
N GETMONTH.COM
A 100
MOV AH, 2A
INT 21
MOV AL, DH
MOV AH, 4C
INT 21
```

(continued)

```
R CX
A
W
Q
```

To create the GETMONTH.COM program, use this command line:

```
C:\> DEBUG < GETMONTH.SCR
```

The GETMONTH utility can be used in any batch file that makes decisions based upon the month. Because GETMONTH returns the month as the ERRORLEVEL value, you must use the GOTO structure shown in SCHEDULE.BAT to control the processing.

FINDING THE DATE

In some cases you might want to run certain commands in a batch file on a specific day of the month, such as the 15th. The following script, GETDAY.SCR, creates the program named GETDAY.COM, which returns an exit-status value that indicates the day of the month:

```
N GETDAY.COM
A 100
MOV AH, 2A
INT 21
MOV AL, DL
MOV AH, 4C
INT 21

R CX
A
W
Q
```

You must use DEBUG to create the actual program from the script:

```
C:\> DEBUG < GETDAY.SCR
```

You can then use GETDAY.COM in a batch file that tests the ERROR-LEVEL value returned by the program and then continues processing accordingly. (We give examples of this technique at the end of this chapter.)

FINDING THE HOUR

The following batch file, GETTIME.BAT, uses a program named GET-HOUR.COM to determine the current hour. The batch file then displays a message based on the hour, as follows:

```
@ECHO OFF
REM Determine the current hour of the day using the
REM GETHOUR.COM program. After the hour is
REM determined, display a message to the user.

GETHOUR

IF ERRORLEVEL  0 IF NOT ERRORLEVEL 6 GOTO TOO_LATE
IF ERRORLEVEL  6 IF NOT ERRORLEVEL 12 GOTO MORNING
IF ERRORLEVEL 12 IF NOT ERRORLEVEL 18 GOTO AFTERNOON
IF ERRORLEVEL 18 GOTO EVENING

:TOO_LATE
ECHO You're up either too late or too early.
GOTO DONE

:MORNING
ECHO Good morning.
GOTO DONE

:AFTERNOON
ECHO Good afternoon.
GOTO DONE

:EVENING
ECHO Good evening. It's getting late.

:DONE
```

GETHOUR.COM uses the following script, GETHOUR.SCR:

```
N GETHOUR.COM
A 100
MOV AH, 2C
INT 21
MOV AL, CH
MOV AH, 4C
INT 21

R CX
A
W
Q
```

As with the previous programs, to create GETHOUR.COM you must use DEBUG as follows:

```
C:\> DEBUG < GETHOUR.SCR
```

The resulting program can be used within any batch file. The value returned in **ERRORLEVEL** represents the current hour on a 24-hour clock. A value of 0 indicates midnight.

FINDING THE MINUTE

This collection of DEBUG utilities would not be complete without one to return the current minute. The following script, GETMIN.SCR, creates a program that returns the minute as an exit-status value in the range 0 through 59:

```
N GETMIN.COM
A 100
MOV AH, 2C
INT 21
MOV AL, CL
MOV AH, 4C
INT 21

R CX
A
W
Q
```

As with our previous examples, to create the actual program, use this:

```
C:\> DEBUG < GETMIN.SCR
```

You now have tools for determining the month, day, hour, and minute when the batch file is processed.

USING THE DATE PROGRAMS

You will find these time and date utilites very useful in creating more complex batch files. For example, you can use these utilities in your AUTOEXEC.BAT file to execute other programs on a given day. On the 15th of each month you might want to automatically invoke the MSAV command to perform virus checking or the DEFRAG command to defragment your hard disk. The following commands illustrate how you might perform this processing:

```
GETDAY
IF ERRORLEVEL 15 IF NOT ERRORLEVEL 16 DEFRAG
IF ERRORLEVEL 15 IF NOT ERRORLEVEL 16 MSAV
```

With these tools in hand you can create some pretty powerful batch files. Experiment with these programs to see how you can automate other routine tasks.

CHAPTER 12

Customizing System Startup—AUTOEXEC.BAT and CONFIG.SYS

TAKING CHARGE USING AUTOEXEC.BAT

Of all the batch files on your hard disk, one stands out as the most important: AUTOEXEC.BAT. Unlike other batch files that you might use once in a while, AUTOEXEC.BAT executes every time your system starts. To ensure that the commands it executes are appropriate for your current configuration, you need to periodically review the contents of your AUTOEXEC.BAT file. This chapter takes a look at a few of the operations you might want to perform from within AUTOEXEC.BAT.

Revisiting the CHOICE Command

As discussed in Chapter 5, MS-DOS versions 6 and later include the CHOICE command, which lets your batch files prompt for a response and then process the response using IF ERRORLEVEL commands. You might want to use CHOICE (with a time-out) in your AUTO-EXEC.BAT file to allow you to indicate at system startup whether you want to run such programs as MSAV (the MS-DOS versions 6 and later virus-detection utility) or DEFRAG (the disk defragmenter), or to install UNDELETE's delete-tracking software. The following commands illustrate how you might use CHOICE with 15-second time-outs within AUTOEXEC.BAT:

```
@ECHO OFF
CHOICE Do you want to run MSAV /T:N,15
IF ERRORLEVEL 1 IF NOT ERRORLEVEL 2 MSAV
CHOICE Do you want to run DEFRAG /T:N,15
IF ERRORLEVEL 1 IF NOT ERRORLEVEL 2 DEFRAG
CHOICE Do you want to install UNDELETE's file-tracking /T:Y,15
IF ERRORLEVEL 1 IF NOT ERRORLEVEL 2 UNDELETE /LOAD
```

If you walk away after turning on your PC, your system responds to the default choices and time-outs by starting without running the MSAV and DEFRAG programs but with delete-tracking installed. Without the defaults, you must be present to respond to each CHOICE prompt.

Using the Date Programs

In Chapter 11, you created the GETMONTH and GETDAY programs. There may be times when you want to use these programs to execute specific commands from within your AUTOEXEC.BAT file on a given day. For example, on the 15th of each month you might want to automatically invoke the MSAV command to perform virus checking and the DEFRAG command to defragment your hard disk. The following commands demonstrate how you might perform this processing:

```
GETDAY
IF ERRORLEVEL 15 IF NOT ERRORLEVEL 16 GOTO 15th
:15th
DEFRAG
MSAV
```

Customizing Your Command Prompt

Many users personalize their systems by changing the command prompt. By default (without the use of the PROMPT command), MS-DOS displays the current disk-drive letter followed by the greater-than symbol (>) as its prompt; for example, C>. However, the installation program for MS-DOS versions 5 and later places a PROMPT command in AUTOEXEC.BAT that directs MS-DOS to display the current directory as the prompt; for example, C:\>. Using the PROMPT command and combinations of *metacharacters*, which consist of the dollar-sign character ($) followed by another character, you can create your own command prompt. PROMPT supports the following metacharacters:

Metacharacter	Corresponding Text
$$	$ character
$b	¦ character
$d	Current system date
$e	ASCII escape character
$g	> character
$h	ASCII backspace character
$l	< character

Metacharacter	Corresponding Text
$n	Current disk drive
$p	Current disk drive and directory
$q	= character
$t	Current system time
$v	Current MS-DOS version
$_	Carriage return/linefeed

NOTE: *In Chapter 8 you learned how to use the $e metacharacter to gener-*
ate escape sequences that direct the ANSI.SYS device driver to set your
screen colors, assign commands to function keys, or to position the cursor so
that your batch files can place menus or other output in specific locations.

After determining how you want your prompt to look, you might consider placing the corresponding PROMPT command in your AUTO-
EXEC.BAT file. For example, the following command displays the
current system date on one line and the current drive and directory
two lines below enclosed in brackets:

```
PROMPT $d$_$_[$p]
```

Assuming that you place this command in AUTOEXEC.BAT, your
prompt lines will resemble the following:

```
Thu 04-07-1994

[C:\DOS]
```

As you can see, MS-DOS displays the current date, followed by the
current directory in square brackets. (Note that the brackets, like any
other characters not preceded by the $ character, are displayed exactly
as entered.) By setting your desired prompt with AUTOEXEC.BAT,
you don't have to remember the necessary PROMPT command line or
enter it each session.

Customizing the PRINT Command

When you work with MS-DOS batch files (or other ASCII files), the
MS-DOS PRINT command provides a convenient way to print a file's
contents. The first time you issue the PRINT command, MS-DOS installs software in your computer's memory that manages your printer
and the files you print. To control this installation, you can include several switches in the command line. These switches specify such prefer-
ences as the selected printer (normally PRN for parallel printers and

COM1 for serial printers); the number of files—from 4 through 32—
that MS-DOS will hold for printing in a list called the *print queue* (the
default is 10); and how much of your computer's time is spent printing
files. The following table briefly describes PRINT's switches:

Switch	Function
/B	Specifies the size of the print buffer.
/C	Cancels one or more files in the print queue.
/D	Specifies the target output device.
/M	Specifies the number of clock ticks during which PRINT can retain control of the printer for each time it begins printing.
/Q	Specifies the number of files the print queue can store.
/S	Specifies the print time slice, which controls how often PRINT gains control of the printer.
/T	Cancels all files in the print queue.
/U	Specifies the number of clock ticks that PRINT can wait for the printer to become available.
/P	Prints the files named on the command line.

NOTE: *The switches that can take parameters can be specified only the first
time PRINT is executed.*

Most people use PRINT's default settings simply because they can't
remember the available switches. In many cases, you can get better
performance from your printer and computer by including a few simple
switches in the PRINT command. AUTOEXEC.BAT provides an easy
way to run PRINT with its optimal settings. For most uses, the following command line will give excellent performance:

```
PRINT /D:PRN /Q:32 /M:64 /U:16 /B:4096
```

If you are using a serial printer connected to the first serial port, change
the /D switch to reference COM1:

```
PRINT /D:COM1 /Q:32 /M:64 /U:16 /B:4096
```

In this case, the /D switch tells PRINT which device to print to. Including this switch suppresses the prompt (*Name of list device [PRN]:*)
that PRINT normally displays the first time you run it. The /Q switch
installs a print queue large enough for 32 files. The /M switch directs
PRINT to retain control of the computer for 64 clock ticks each time it
begins printing. The /U switch directs PRINT to retain control for 16
clock ticks while waiting for the printer to become available (if the

printer is currently busy). Lastly the /B switch sets aside a print buffer of 4096 bytes. PRINT fills this buffer with characters from the file each time it reads from disk. Because this buffer is quite large (the default is 512 bytes), the number of slow disk-input operations PRINT must perform to print a file is reduced. Reducing disk-input operations improves overall system performance.

Disk Caching Using SMARTDRV.EXE

Compared with the speed of your computer's electronic components, your disk is very slow. One way to improve performance is to reduce the number of disk read or write operations MS-DOS must perform. If your computer contains extended memory, you can improve your system performance by installing SMARTDRV's disk-caching support. In general, SMARTDRV uses a section of your computer's extended memory as a buffer called a *cache* so that the number of slow disk read and write operations your computer must perform is reduced. Depending on how much extended memory your computer has, your SMARTDRV entry in AUTOEXEC.BAT will vary. However, the following command should improve performance for a system with 2 to 4 MB of extended memory.

```
SMARTDRV C+ 1024
```

In this case, SMARTDRV uses a 1-MB disk cache and performs read and write caching for drive C.

Be sure your CONFIG.SYS file installs a device driver to manage extended memory so that it is accessible to SMARTDRV. If you are using MS-DOS version 5 or later, the following CONFIG.SYS entry installs the HIMEM.SYS driver:

```
DEVICE=C:\DOS\HIMEM.SYS
```

Remember: DEVICE= entries are CONFIG.SYS entries, not commands that you place in AUTOEXEC.BAT.

Improving Directory Search Operations Using FASTOPEN

If your system does not have extended memory, you can use the FAST-OPEN command rather than SMARTDRV. The FASTOPEN command reduces the amount of time MS-DOS spends searching your disk for files that you use on a regular basis. Each time you open, print, or copy a file, MS-DOS normally reads your disk looking for the file's directory entry. When MS-DOS locates the directory entry, it determines the file's size and where the file is stored on disk. The FASTOPEN command installs memory-resident software that keeps track of the files you use, placing a copy of the file's directory entry in a buffer in memory. When you open a file, MS-DOS first checks FASTOPEN's buffer for the file's directory entry. If the buffer contains the entry, MS-DOS does not have to search the slow disk for it. If the buffer does not contain the entry, MS-DOS reads the entry from disk, placing a copy in FASTOPEN's buffer so that the next time you use the file, MS-DOS can find the entry in the buffer. If the buffer is full, the oldest entry is replaced.

The FASTOPEN command doesn't improve system performance for every file you use, but rather for the files you repeatedly use. The following FASTOPEN command directs MS-DOS to track up to 75 files on drive C:

```
FASTOPEN C:=75
```

Using the LOADHIGH Command

If you are using MS-DOS version 5 or later with a 386 or higher microprocessor, you can take advantage of the 384-KB range of memory located between 640 KB and 1 MB that is called *reserved* or *upper memory*. To use upper memory, you need the following entries in your CONFIG.SYS file:

```
DEVICE=C:\DOS\HIMEM.SYS
DEVICE=C:\DOS\EMM386.EXE NOEMS
DOS=UMB
```

These statements enable MS-DOS to access and manage upper memory. Your exact configuration might vary (for example, it might not have the NOEMS parameter). After you install support for upper memory, you can load device drivers and memory-resident programs into this memory, freeing up your system's conventional memory for use by MS-DOS and your MS-DOS programs. To load device drivers into upper memory, you use the DEVICEHIGH= entry in your CONFIG.SYS file. For example, the following entry loads the ANSI.SYS device driver into upper memory:

```
DEVICEHIGH=C:\DOS\ANSI.SYS
```

To load memory-resident programs (and memory-resident DOS commands) into upper memory, you use the LOADHIGH command. For example, the following LOADHIGH commands load the PRINT and SMARTDRV programs into upper memory:

```
LOADHIGH C:\DOS\PRINT /D:PRN /Q:32
LOADHIGH C:\DOS\SMARTDRV C+ 1024
```

Scanning Your Disk for Computer Viruses

MS-DOS versions 6 and later provides the MSAV command, which scans your disk for and removes computer viruses. You can use MSAV in two ways: first, by choosing commands and selecting the desired drives and operations in MSAV's graphical user interface; and second, by using command-line switches, much as you would with any MS-DOS command. If you often download files from computer bulletin boards or exchange floppy disks with other users, you should frequently test your disk for viruses. The following command runs MSAV to scan for, and remove, any viruses on C: using the second method:

```
MSAV C: /C
```

You could put this command line in your AUTOEXEC.BAT file. However, depending on the number of files stored on your disk, the amount of processing time MSAV requires varies, and you might not want MSAV to run every time your system starts. By using the CHOICE command, you can have AUTOEXEC.BAT ask you whether you want to run MSAV. If you respond by pressing Y (for Yes), AUTOEXEC.BAT invokes MSAV; otherwise, it doesn't.

Enabling Delete-Tracking

Beginning with version 5, MS-DOS provides the UNDELETE command, which lets you restore accidentally deleted files. To improve UNDELETE's chances of recovering files in version 5, most MS-DOS 5 users installed delete-tracking support by placing a MIRROR command similar to the following in their AUTOEXEC.BAT files:

```
MIRROR C: /TC
```

MS-DOS versions 6 and later do not support the MIRROR command. To enable delete-tracking under these versions, you must load the UNDELETE file-tracking software, as shown here:

```
UNDELETE /LOAD
```

The type of file tracking is determined by the settings in the UNDE-LETE.INI file. You use command-line switches (or the UNDELETE utility) to configure the protection level. If you have a large amount of free disk space, you can invoke UNDELETE with the maximum-security Delete Sentry protection, also available with MS-DOS versions 6 and later.

Improving Your Keyboard's Response Rate

The MODE command lets you control your keyboard's responsiveness. MODE works with two different keyboard settings: the typematic rate and the typematic delay. The typematic rate specifies the number of times the key repeats per second. The typematic delay specifies the length of time you must hold down a key before the keystroke repeats.

The PC supports the 32 typematic rates listed here:

Typematic Rate	Characters per Second	Typematic Rate	Characters per Second
1	2.0	17	8.4
2	2.1	18	8.6
3	2.3	19	9.2
4	2.5	20	10.0
5	2.7	21	10.9
6	3.0	22	12.0
7	3.3	23	13.3
8	3.7	24	15.0
9	4.0	25	16.0
10	4.3	26	17.1
11	4.6	27	18.5
12	5.0	28	20.0
13	5.5	29	21.8
14	6.0	30	24.0
15	6.7	31	26.7
16	7.5	32	30.0

The four typematic delays supported by the PC are listed in the following table.

Typematic Delay	Delay in Seconds	Typematic Delay	Delay in Seconds
1	¼	3	¾
2	½	4	1

The following MODE command sets the keyboard to its maximum responsiveness:

```
MODE CON DELAY=1 RATE=32
```

SETTING UP YOUR SYSTEM WITH CONFIG.SYS

MS-DOS provides the means to control your system startup by customizing your CONFIG.SYS file. As discussed in Chapter 2, your CONFIG.SYS file contains configuration commands that determine how MS-DOS installs itself in memory. CONFIG.SYS is not a batch file, and the only time MS-DOS uses CONFIG.SYS is when you start your system, so if you make a change to CONFIG.SYS, you must reboot your system for the change to take effect.

The following file demonstrates some typical CONFIG.SYS entries:

```
DEVICE=C:\DOS\SETVER.EXE
DEVICE=C:\DOS\HIMEM.SYS
DEVICE=C:\DOS\EMM386.EXE NOEMS
DOS=HIGH,UMB
DEVICEHIGH=C:\DOS\ANSI.SYS
FILES=50
BUFFERS=30
```

Depending on your MS-DOS version, the entries in your CONFIG.SYS file will differ. Chapter 2 describes the possible CONFIG.SYS entries.

If you use your computer as a regular part of your job, you probably work with different application programs that have different MS-DOS requirements. For example, when you use a database program, MS-DOS might have to open many different files and perform many disk read and write operations. When you use a word-processing program, MS-DOS might have to reserve a large amount of conventional memory for the program's use. As you will learn in this chapter, MS-DOS versions 6 and later let you customize your CONFIG.SYS file so that it supports many different configurations. When your system starts, you can have MS-DOS display a menu of startup options from which you can select the desired configuration.

You don't use MS-DOS batch files to create the startup menu. Instead, you use special CONFIG.SYS entries supported only by MS-DOS 6 and later.

Basic Control over CONFIG.SYS and AUTOEXEC.BAT

Later in this chapter you will learn how to create a startup menu that lets you select specific startup options, similiar to the one shown here:

```
MS-DOS 6.2 Startup Menu
═══════════════════════

    1. Configure for high-memory use
    2. Configure for network
    3. Configure for database

Enter a choice: 1
```

In the meantime, however, you can use the F5 and F8 keys to control how MS-DOS processes CONFIG.SYS.

Each time your system starts, MS-DOS first processes the CONFIG.SYS entries that tell it how to configure itself in memory. MS-DOS then executes the commands contained in your AUTOEXEC.BAT file. There may be times, however, when you don't want MS-DOS to process the CONFIG.SYS entries or execute the commands in AUTOEXEC.BAT. With MS-DOS versions 6 and later, each time your system starts you see the message *Starting MS-DOS*. If you press the F5 key immediately after this message appears, MS-DOS does not process CONFIG.SYS or execute the commands in AUTOEXEC.BAT.

NOTE: *If you press the F5 key, MS-DOS ignores CONFIG.SYS and AUTO-EXEC.BAT, and your system starts with a minimal configuration. For example, your search path will contain only C:\DOS, not the path defined in AUTOEXEC.BAT.*

Bypassing CONFIG.SYS and AUTOEXEC.BAT

There may be times when you want MS-DOS to bypass the processing of CONFIG.SYS and AUTOEXEC.BAT. For example, assume that you have changed one of the files and the change prevents your system from starting. By rebooting your system and pressing the F5 key, you can get your system up and running, and you can then edit the file to correct or remove the change.

If you want MS-DOS to process some CONFIG.SYS and AUTO-
EXEC.BAT entries while ignoring others, press the F8 key after MS-
DOS displays its startup message. MS-DOS then prompts you to press
Y or N to specify whether you want it to process or ignore each entry.

For example, suppose that the first two lines in your CONFIG.SYS file
contain the following entries:

```
DEVICE=C:\DOS\SETVER.EXE
DEVICE=C:\DOS\HIMEM.SYS
```

If you press the F8 key immediately after MS-DOS starts, you can
choose whether MS-DOS processes the commands by responding with
a Y or N to the [Y,N] prompt, as shown here:

```
DEVICE=C:\DOS\SETVER.EXE [Y,N]?N
DEVICE=C:\DOS\HIMEM.SYS [Y,N]?Y
```

In this case, MS-DOS would not process the SETVER.EXE entry but
would process the HIMEM.SYS entry.

After you have responded to prompts for each of the commands in
CONFIG.SYS, MS-DOS asks whether you want it to execute the commands in your AUTOEXEC.BAT file:

```
Process AUTOEXEC.BAT [Y,N]?
```

If you press N, MS-DOS does not process any of the AUTO-
EXEC.BAT commands and immediately displays the command
prompt. If you press Y, MS-DOS executes the commands in the AUTO-
EXEC.BAT file. MS-DOS version 6.2 also allows you to choose
whether you want to process each entry. Press Y if you would like MS-
DOS to execute the command. Press N to skip the command.

Processing Each CONFIG.SYS and AUTOEXEC.BAT Entry

There may be times when you want MS-DOS to selectively process
your CONFIG.SYS and AUTOEXEC.BAT entries. When MS-DOS displays its startup message, you can press the F8 key to have MS-DOS
prompt you to press Y to process each entry or N to ignore the entry.
After you specify the desired processing for each CONFIG.SYS entry,
MS-DOS prompts you to indicate whether you want it to execute the
commands in your AUTOEXEC.BAT file.

NOTE: *The F8 key option exists primarily to enable you to get your system started when a CONFIG.SYS entry or AUTOEXEC.BAT command is preventing successful startup.*

Creating System Configuration Menus

Earlier in this chapter, you learned how to use the CHOICE command to control the execution of commands in your AUTOEXEC.BAT file. You have also learned that, by pressing the F5 key when your system starts, you can produce similar Y/N prompts for your CONFIG.SYS entries. Although this entry-by-entry prompting lets you control which entries MS-DOS processes, answering prompts can be time-consuming if your CONFIG.SYS file contains many entries.

Depending on the application programs you use, you might have more than one CONFIG.SYS file that you use on a regular basis. For example, if you work on a network, you might use one CONFIG.SYS file that installs various network device drivers. When you are not working on the network, however, you might want to use a different CON-FIG.SYS to free up conventional memory so that you can run a large application program, such as a database. For a third configuration, you might have a third CONFIG.SYS file. In the past, the easiest way to change configurations was to create files with names like CON-FIG.NOR (for normal operations where you want access to the maximum amount of memory), CONFIG.NET (for network), and CON-FIG.DBS (for database). Then when you needed a specific setup, you would simply copy the desired file's contents to CONFIG.SYS and reboot your computer. For example, the following COPY command would copy the entries for the network configuration to CONFIG.SYS:

```
C:\> COPY CONFIG.NET CONFIG.SYS
```

With MS-DOS versions 6 and later, you no longer have to manage multiple CONFIG.SYS files. MS-DOS provides CONFIG.SYS entries that allow you to create a menu of options from which you can select the desired configuration.

Here is a list of the MS-DOS versions 6 and later CONFIG.SYS customization entries:

Entry	Purpose
MENUCOLOR	Specifies the foreground and background color of the CONFIG.SYS startup menu.
MENUITEM	Specifies an option that appears in the CONFIG.SYS startup menu.
MENUDEFAULT	Specifies the default option for the CONFIG.SYS startup menu.
INCLUDE	Includes startup entries specified in one configuration block within another block.
SUBMENU	Specifies a submenu of startup options.

To use these entries to customize your system configuration, you divide your CONFIG.SYS file into blocks of entries. For example, you might place the entries needed for a network configuration in one block, and the entries needed for a database application in another.

Each block you create within CONFIG.SYS has a unique name enclosed in square brackets, such as [BlockName]. Block names can contain up to 70 characters. For example, you might have blocks named [HighMemory], [Network], and [Database].

Each of the three configurations (HighMemory, the normal configuration; Network; and Database) requires its own set of commands. If they are organized into separate blocks, the CONFIG.SYS file would contain the following:

```
[HighMemory]
FILES=50
BUFFERS=30
DEVICE=C:\DOS\HIMEM.SYS
DEVICE=C:\DOS\EMM386.EXE NOEMS
DOS=HIGH,UMB

[Network]
FILES=50
BUFFERS=30
DEVICE=C:\NETDRIVE.EXE
DEVICE=C:\NETPRINT.EXE

[Database]
FILES=50
BUFFERS=30
DEVICE=RAMDRIVE.SYS 512
DEVICE=DBCACHE.SYS
```

Usually you will have several entries that are common to all the blocks, such as BUFFERS=, FILES=, and frequently used DEVICE= entries.

To avoid repetition of these entries in each block, you can define special blocks named [COMMON] within which you can place such entries. You can create more than one [COMMON] block, and very often your CONFIG.SYS file will start and end with such a block. Installation programs will add new entries to the final [COMMON] block. MS-DOS performs the entries listed in these blocks regardless of the configuration option you select. For example, the following CONFIG.SYS file contains four blocks, one containing entries common to the other three blocks, one for the normal high-memory utilization, one for a network configuration, and one for database operations:

```
[COMMON]
FILES=50
BUFFERS=30

[HighMemory]
DEVICE=C:\DOS\HIMEM.SYS
DEVICE=C:\DOS\EMM386.EXE NOEMS
DOS=HIGH,UMB

[Network]
DEVICE=C:\NETDRIVE.EXE
DEVICE=C:\NETPRINT.EXE

[Database]
DEVICE=RAMDRIVE.SYS 512
DEVICE=DBCACHE.SYS
```

After you define the different configurations, you need a way to select one of them at system startup. You do this by creating a startup menu using MENUITEM entries in CONFIG.SYS. Each MENUITEM entry specifies an option that appears in a startup menu and identifies the block of entries that MS-DOS processes if you choose that option. In each MENUITEM entry, you specify the block name and any text that is to appear in the startup menu, as shown here:

MENUITEM=BlockName[,MenuText]

For example, the following entries create options for the high-memory use, network, and database configurations:

```
[MENU]
MENUITEM=HighMemory,Configure for high-memory use
MENUITEM=Network,Configure for network
MENUITEM=Database,Configure for database
```

As you can see, you place the MENUITEM entries within a special block named [MENU]. When you combine the entries with the configuration blocks shown earlier, CONFIG.SYS looks as follows:

```
[MENU]
MENUITEM=HighMemory,Configure for high-memory use
MENUITEM=Network,Configure for network
MENUITEM=Database,Configure for database

[COMMON]
FILES=50
BUFFERS=30

[HighMemory]
DEVICE=C:\DOS\HIMEM.SYS
DEVICE=C:\DOS\EMM386.EXE NOEMS
DOS=HIGH,UMB

[Network]
DEVICE=C:\NETDRIVE.EXE
DEVICE=C:\NETPRINT.EXE

[Database]
DEVICE=RAMDRIVE.SYS 512
DEVICE=DBCACHE.SYS
```

When you start a system containing this CONFIG.SYS file, MS-DOS displays the following menu on your screen:

```
MS-DOS 6.2 Startup Menu
═══════════════════════

    1. Configure for high-memory use
    2. Configure for network
    3. Configure for database

Enter a choice: 1
```

To select a menu option, simply type the option's number or highlight the option using the arrow keys, and then press Enter.

Using descriptive menu text within the MENUITEM entry is optional. If you don't specify any text, MS-DOS displays the block name in the startup menu. For example, the following menu does not include any descriptive text:

```
[MENU]
MENUITEM=HighMemory
MENUITEM=Network
MENUITEM=Database
```

When your system starts, MS-DOS displays the following:

```
MS-DOS 6.2 Startup Menu
════════════════════════

    1. HighMemory
    2. Network
    3. Database

Enter a choice: 1
```

Controlling the Startup Menu's Color

By default, MS-DOS displays the startup menu in black and white. To help you further customize your system startup, the CONFIG.SYS MENUCOLOR entry lets you specify the color of the startup menu. The format of this entry is as follows:

MENUCOLOR=ForegroundColor[,BackgroundColor]

The foreground and background colors are specified using color values from 0 through 15, as listed in the following table:

Color Value	Color	Color Value	Color
0	Black	8	Gray
1	Blue	9	Bright blue
2	Green	10	Bright green
3	Cyan	11	Bright cyan
4	Red	12	Bright red
5	Magenta	13	Bright magenta
6	Brown	14	Yellow
7	White	15	Bright white

For example, the following entry directs MS-DOS to display bright red menu text on a blue background:

```
[MENU]
MENUCOLOR=12,1
MENUITEM=HighMemory,Configure for high-memory use
MENUITEM=Network,Configure for network
MENUITEM=Database,Configure for database
```

Selecting a Default Menu Option

As you learned earlier, when you include CHOICE commands in your AUTOEXEC.BAT file, your computer waits for keyboard responses instead of completing its startup. In a similiar way, when you include MENUITEM entries in your CONFIG.SYS file, your system won't start unless you are at the keyboard to select the desired option. With the CHOICE command, you can define a default option and time-out period; the same is true for the MENUITEM entries.

You might have noticed that the startup menus previously shown display the first menu option as the default choice. Depending on your configuration settings, you might want to select a different option as the default. In addition, you might want to specify a time-out period from 0 to 90 seconds after which MS-DOS will automatically select the default option. By including a time-out, you can ensure that your system starts, even if you are away from the keyboard.

The CONFIG.SYS MENUDEFAULT entry lets you specify the default option as well as the time-out period. The format of the MENU-DEFAULT entry is as follows:

    MENUDEFAULT=BlockName[,Time-outPeriod]

For example, the following MENUDEFAULT entry tells MS-DOS to select the Network configuration if another option is not selected within 45 seconds:

```
[MENU]
MENUDEFAULT=Network,45
MENUITEM=HighMemory,Configure for high-memory use
MENUITEM=Network,Configure for network
MENUITEM=Database,Configure for database
```

When you specify a default option and time-out, MS-DOS displays a countdown of the number of seconds remaining until it selects the option, as shown here:

```
MS-DOS 6.2 Startup Menu
═══════════════════════

    1. Configure for high-memory use
    2. Select network configuration
    3. Select database configuration

Enter a choice: 2          Time remaining: 25
```

A time-out of zero (0) causes the menu to be bypassed.

Including One Block's Entries Within Another Block

To configure the CONFIG.SYS file using the startup-menu entries, you divide the file into multiple blocks. Depending upon how you group your menu entries, one block might contain entries that are also contained in another block. Rather than duplicating the entries, you can use the INCLUDE entry to include the second block's entries. The format of INCLUDE is as follows:

INCLUDE=BlockName

For example, assume that you want to modify the [Network] block to take advantage of upper memory. You could add the entries shown here:

```
[Network]
DEVICE=C:\DOS\HIMEM.SYS
DEVICE=C:\DOS\EMM386.EXE NOEMS
DOS=HIGH,UMB
DEVICEHIGH=C:\NETDRIVE.EXE
DEVICEHIGH=C:\NETPRINT.EXE
```

As you can see, the first three entries in the [Network] block are the same as those defined in [HighMemory]. Rather than duplicate the entries, you can include the [HighMemory] entries within [Network], as shown here:

```
[MENU]
MENUITEM=HighMemory,Configure for high-memory use
MENUITEM=Network,Configure for network
MENUITEM=Database,Configure for database

[COMMON]
FILES=50
BUFFERS=30

[HighMemory]
DEVICE=C:\DOS\HIMEM.SYS
DEVICE=C:\DOS\EMM386.EXE NOEMS
DOS=HIGH,UMB

[Network]
INCLUDE=HighMemory
DEVICEHIGH=C:\NETDRIVE.EXE
DEVICEHIGH=C:\NETPRINT.EXE

[Database]
DEVICE=RAMDRIVE.SYS 512
DEVICE=DBCACHE.SYS
```

Creating Several Menu Levels

As your system configurations become more complex, there may be times when you can't easily present the different configuration options using only one menu. You'll then want to consider using the

SUBMENU entry, which lets you specify another level of menus. The format of the SUBMENU entry is as follows:

SUBMENU=MenuBlock[,MenuText]

MenuBlock specifies the name of the CONFIG.SYS block that contains the additional level of MENUITEM entries. When your system starts, MS-DOS first finds the [MENU] block and displays the entries it contains. If you select an option that corresponds to a submenu, MS-DOS displays a second menu, followed possibly by a third or fourth.

Assume, for example, that if you select the database option, you want MS-DOS to ask whether you want to also load your network software. The following CONFIG.SYS file uses the SUBMENU entry to do that:

```
[MENU]
MENUITEM=HighMemory,Configure for high-memory use
MENUITEM=Network,Configure for network
SUBMENU=AskNetwork,Configure for database

[COMMON]
FILES=50
BUFFERS=30

[HighMemory]
DEVICE=C:\DOS\HIMEM.SYS
DEVICE=C:\DOS\EMM386.EXE NOEMS
DOS=HIGH,UMB

[Network]
DEVICE=C:\NETDRIVE.EXE
DEVICE=C:\NETPRINT.EXE

[Database]
DEVICE=RAMDRIVE.SYS 512
DEVICE=DBCACHE.SYS

[AskNetwork]
MENUITEM=DBNoNet,Do not load network
MENUITEM=DBNet,Configure for network

[DBNoNet]
INCLUDE=Database

[DBNet]
INCLUDE=Network
INCLUDE=Database
```

As you can see, the [MENU] block contains a SUBMENU entry that selects a second level of menu options. When the system starts, MS-DOS
displays the following:

```
MS-DOS 6.2 Startup Menu
═══════════════════════

    1. Configure for high-memory use
    2. Configure for network
    3. Configure for database

Enter a choice: 1
```

If you select option 3, MS-DOS displays a second menu of options, as
shown here:

```
MS-DOS 6.2 Startup Menu
═══════════════════════

    1. Do not load network
    2. Configure for network

Enter a choice: 1
```

If you select option 1, MS-DOS branches to the [DBNoNet] block,
which uses the existing [Database] block to configure the system. If
you select option 2, MS-DOS branches to the [DBNet] block and uses
the [Network] and [Database] blocks. In this example, the submenu entries rely upon existing blocks from the original menu, however, this
does not have to be the case. A SUBMENU command references a
block that contains MENUITEM entries (as well as optional MENU-
DEFAULT and MENUCOLOR entries). These MENUITEM entries
reference blocks in the same way they would if they were on the main
menu. The blocks can contain any valid CONFIG.SYS command including additional SUBMENU and INCLUDE statements.

INTERACTION BETWEEN CONFIG.SYS AND AUTOEXEC.BAT

There will be times when you want the commands in your AUTO-
EXEC.BAT file to vary depending on the configuration selected at system startup. By default, MS-DOS assigns to the CONFIG environment
variable the name of the configuration block selected from the startup
menu. Using the previous CONFIG.SYS example, the CONFIG environment variable might contain the value HighMemory, Network,

DBNoNet, or DBNet. Within your AUTOEXEC.BAT file, you can use the %CONFIG% named parameter to determine the current setting of the CONFIG environment variable, as shown here:

```
IF %CONFIG%==HighMemory GOTO HIGH_MEMORY_COMMANDS
IF %CONFIG%==Database GOTO DATABASE_COMMANDS
IF %CONFIG%==Network GOTO NETWORK_COMMANDS
```

Using SET from Within CONFIG.SYS

As discussed in Chapter 6, you can use the SET command to assign values to the MS-DOS environment variables. Beginning with MS-DOS versions 6 and later, you can use SET in your CONFIG.SYS file. Based upon the configuration selected at system startup, you can assign values to environment variables in CONFIG.SYS that you can test from within AUTOEXEC.BAT. For example, depending on your computer's memory configuration, you might create an environment variable called SMART_DRIVE that contains either the value INSTALLED or the value NOT_INSTALLED, as shown here:

```
[HighMemory]
DEVICE=C:\DOS\HIMEM.SYS
DEVICE=C:\DOS\EMM386.EXE NOEMS
DOS=HIGH,UMB
DEVICE=C:\DOS\SMARTDRV.EXE
SET SMART_DRIVE=INSTALLED
```

Later, within AUTOEXEC.BAT, you can test the variable's value as shown here:

```
IF "%SMART_DRIVE%"=="INSTALLED" SomeCommand
```

CHAPTER 13

Batch Files and Microsoft Windows

AUTOEXEC.BAT AND WINDOWS

Although most people don't really think about MS-DOS batch files when they run Microsoft Windows, MS-DOS does provide some batch-file capabilities that you may want to consider. This section takes a brief look at a few of these capabilities.

One of the most important things to remember about Windows is that it forms an operating environment on top of MS-DOS. This means that the way you configure MS-DOS affects the way Windows performs. This fact is obvious when you consider device drivers and other configuration commands (such as SmartDrive), but there are also more subtle interactions. For example, two environment entries that you can set in AUTOEXEC.BAT are particularly important to Windows.

The first of these entries is TEMP, which determines the drive used by Windows for temporary files. Although you don't have to specify a TEMP drive, it is generally a good idea. Here's how you tell Windows to store temporary files on your D drive:

```
SET TEMP=D:
```

You can often improve your system's performance by assigning TEMP to a RAM drive.

Windows 3.1 users can take advantage of WINPMT, the second important environment entry, which sets the command prompt for MS-DOS sessions within Windows. The following entry sets the WINPMT environment entry to the message *Temporary MS-DOS* followed by the current directory name inside brackets:

```
SET WINPMT=Temporary MS-DOS [$p]
```

When you start an MS-DOS session from within Windows, the prompt includes the message and path information. The *Temporary MS-DOS* message reminds you that you're running an MS-DOS session from within Windows and that you must use the EXIT command to return to Windows. This technique allows you to specify one prompt for use in MS-DOS (with the PROMPT command) and another for use in MS-DOS sessions within Windows (with the WINPMT environment entry).

USING WINSTART.BAT

As you know, each time MS-DOS starts, it executes the AUTO-EXEC.BAT batch file. In a similar way, when you first start Windows in 386 enhanced mode, Windows executes a special batch file named WINSTART.BAT. Although you can use WINSTART.BAT just as you would any MS-DOS batch file, this batch file's primary purpose is to configure the environment for Windows-based applications. As a result, you can have two environments: one for use by Windows-based applications and one for MS-DOS sessions. When you start an MS-DOS session from within Windows, Windows duplicates the MS-DOS environment that was in effect before WINSTART.BAT was executed.

Just as you can modify AUTOEXEC.BAT to configure your environment for your MS-DOS sessions, you can modify WINSTART.BAT to configure the Windows environment. For example, depending on the Windows-based applications you use, you might want to change the search path to eliminate some directories (those with MS-DOS–specific programs) and include others. Likewise, you might want to unload MS-DOS–based memory-resident programs (TSRs) before Windows starts and add Windows-based TSRs. Regardless of the operations you need to perform, you can place the necessary commands in WIN-START.BAT.

Modifying the Search Path for Windows

As briefly discussed in Chapter 2, when you add directories to your search path, you should ensure that the directories are likely to contain your commonly used commands. The more directories you add to the search path, the more time MS-DOS must spend searching through the directories' contents. As you know, the WINDOWS directory and the directories for your Windows-based applications contain a large number of files. As a rule, you should add these directories to your search path only when you are ready to use Windows.

One way to add these directories to your search path is to redefine the path in the WINSTART.BAT file. The following entry provides a typical path for Windows:

```
PATH C:\WINDOWS;C:\DOS;C:\EXCEL;C:\WINWORD
```

This entry assumes that your files are located on drive C and installed in the default directories. Keep in mind that the path changes only for the Windows environment. For MS-DOS sessions, the path defined before you entered the command to start Windows is still in effect.

Another option is to create a batch file for starting Windows. You can then control the environment in effect when you start Windows and reset the environment when you exit Windows. The environment in effect when you start Windows with your own batch file is global—it affects both the Windows environment and the MS-DOS environment— whereas the changes made by WINSTART.BAT do not affect your MS-DOS sessions.

The following batch file, WINDOWS.BAT, saves the current search path as the OLD_PATH environment entry. The batch file then adds three directories to the path and invokes Windows. After you exit Windows, the batch file restores the original search path:

```
@ECHO OFF
SET OLD_PATH=%PATH%
PATH C:\WINDOWS;C:\EXCEL;C:\WINWORD;%PATH%
WIN
PATH %OLD_PATH%
SET OLD_PATH=
```

Place this batch file in a directory on your search path. When you want to use Windows, invoke WINDOWS.BAT like this:

```
C:\> WINDOWS
```

USING BATCH FILES WITHIN WINDOWS

In Windows, a program item is an icon in Program Manager that corresponds to a specific program. Using the Program Manager's File menu, you can create icons for your batch files. To do this, follow these steps:

1. Be sure the group to which you want to add the new icon is active.
2. Choose New from the Program Manager's File menu.
3. When Windows displays the New Program Object dialog box, select Program Item and press Enter.

4. When Windows displays the Program Item Properties dialog box (shown in Figure 13-1), type the name you want to appear beneath the icon and press the Tab key once. In the Command Line text box, type the complete path of the batch file and any parameters you want passed to the batch file.

5. Select OK. The icon of your newly created program item should appear in the current group window. Using a mouse, you can now double-click the icon to invoke the batch file.

FIGURE 13-1. *The Program Item Properties dialog box.*

The advantages of using batch files from within Windows might not be obvious at first, but they can serve a variety of useful purposes. Two of the most common purposes are to control the environment for a specific program and to customize the environment for an MS-DOS session. Of course, just being able to access your batch files with an icon is an important first step.

Using Batch Files to Start Programs

The most important thing to remember about using batch files within Windows is that any changes that the batch file makes to the environment are in effect only during that specific MS-DOS session. If you run more than one MS-DOS session, each session has its own environment. When the MS-DOS session is over, the changes vanish. Of course, the results of actions performed in that one session (such as deleting a file) are permanent.

You can use this environment limitation to your advantage by creating batch files to start your MS-DOS applications from within Windows. Some of the changes you might want to make to the environment include modifying the path, switching to a startup directory, or loading a TSR for use with a particular program. (Remember, the TSR will be available only during that MS-DOS session. If you want to have access to the TSR during all MS-DOS sessions, you must load it before starting

Windows.) The following batch file demonstrates using this technique to start Microsoft Word:

```
@ECHO OFF
PATH=C:\WORD;%PATH%
CD \LETTERS
CALCIT
WORD
```

If you use Microsoft Word only from within Windows, you do not need to add its directory to your search path. In this example, CALCIT is a fictitious TSR that is loaded before starting the Word program. Because the changes are unique to each Word session, you don't have to worry about resetting them when you quit Word. When you quit, you also exit the MS-DOS session, and the environment vanishes.

NOTE: *In general, when you exit the MS-DOS application, the MS-DOS session is over, and you return to Windows. However, some TSRs prevent Windows from recognizing that you have ended the session, and you will have to use the EXIT command to return to Windows.*

Creating a Custom MS-DOS Session

In MS-DOS versions 6 and later, the COMMAND command has a new /K switch that allows you to specify a batch file or program to be executed each time you load a new instance of the COMMAND.COM command processor. One of the most powerful uses of this feature is for customizing MS-DOS sessions within Windows.

The first step is to create a batch file that contains commands for configuring the environment. The following batch file, WINEXEC.BAT, contains some typical entries:

```
PROMPT Custom MS-DOS ($p)
PATH C:\DOS;C:\BATCH;C:\PROGRAM
SET TEMP=D:
```

This batch file uses the PROMPT and PATH commands to configure the basic environment. Then it assigns the TEMP directory to drive D.

Using the /K switch, you can now create an icon in Program Manager that you can double-click to start an MS-DOS session with the custom environment. Assuming that your batch files are located in a directory called BATCH on drive C, the entry for the Command Line text box in the Program Item Properties dialog box is as follows:

```
C:\DOS\COMMAND.COM /K C:\BATCH\WINEXEC.BAT
```

When you double-click the new icon, WINEXEC.BAT configures the environment used by the new instance of COMMAND.COM, which is similar to the way that AUTOEXEC.BAT configures your intial MS-DOS environment.

Although other techniques are available, this is the most efficient way to customize an MS-DOS session. You can include any type of command in the batch file, but the most common are configuration commands and TSRs.

In MS-DOS versions earlier than 6, the best method is to start a plain MS-DOS session and then run a batch file that makes all necessary changes to the environment. You end up with the same environment you would have with MS-DOS versions 6 and later. The only difference is that you have to manually run the batch file.

ADVANCED WINDOWS BATCH-FILE MANAGEMENT

Creating a program item that references a batch file is the simplest way to assign an icon to a batch file, but it doesn't provide much control. For greater control over your batch file, you need to develop a program information file (PIF) from within Windows. A PIF is a special file that defines the relationship between Windows and an MS-DOS session (and the applications running within that session). Standard MS-DOS sessions within Windows are controlled by a PIF named DOSPRMPT.PIF. Modifying this PIF changes the relationship for MS-DOS sessions initiated by double-clicking the MS-DOS Prompt icon.

To create a PIF, start Windows' PIF Editor program by double-clicking its icon. (By default, this icon is in the Main group.) If you are running Windows in enhanced mode, you then see the dialog box shown in Figure 13-2 on the next page. If you are in standard mode, the dialog box is slightly different, but the settings discussed here are the same.

The only entry that you must specify is the name of the batch file in the Program Filename text box. You can use the default values for all of the other settings, but the advantage of creating a PIF is the greater control you can achieve by customizing these settings. (In a moment, we'll look at two of these options: passing optional parameters and controlling the output.)

After you have created the PIF, you must save it and then create a program item for it so that it is represented by an icon in Program

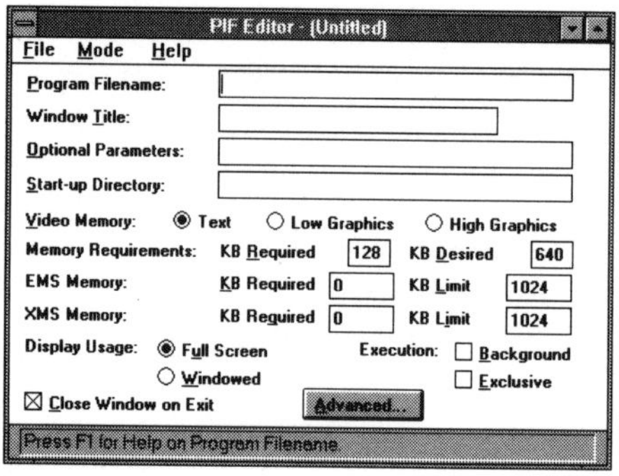

FIGURE 13-2. *The PIF Editor dialog box.*

Manager. Follow the steps described earlier for creating a program item
for a batch file, but enter the PIF filename in the Command Line text
box instead of the name of the batch file. (By default, PIFs are stored
in the WINDOWS directory.)

Passing Parameters to Batch Files

As you learned earlier, the ability to specify parameters enables you to
create more flexible batch files. When using batch files within Windows,
two techniques are available for specifying parameter values.

When you create a PIF for a batch file, you can include the values to be
used for each parameter in the Optional Parameters text box. It is usually easiest to create several PIFs that reference the same batch file,
each with a different set of parameter values. For example, suppose you
have written the CLEANUP.BAT batch file, which searches your hard
disk for files with a specific extension and then deletes those files. You
then create separate PIFs for each type of file you want deleted. In this
case, you create one for all files with the TMP extension and another
for those with the BAK extension. Assuming that the batch file requires
you to specify the extension as the %1 parameter, both PIFs in this example have the same Command Line entry, but one specifies the TMP
extension in the Optional Parameters text box and the other specifies
BAK. If you use this technique, be sure to give each PIF a different
name and each PIF's icon a name that describes its use.

NOTE: *You can also specify a specific parameter value in the Command Line entry when using the Program Item Properties dialog box to assign an icon to a batch file. Using this method, you can create different icons for each task without having to develop a PIF.*

The second approach is to enter a question mark in the PIF Editor's Optional Parameters text box. Then when you double-click the batch file's icon in Program Manager, a dialog box similar to the one shown in Figure 13-3 is displayed.

FIGURE 13-3. *The dialog box displayed when the Optional Parameters entry is a question mark.*

The first value you enter in the dialog box's Parameters text box is passed to the batch file as the %1 parameter. If you include more than one value, the remaining values are passed to the batch file as additional parameters (%2, %3, and so on).

Controlling Batch-File Output

By default, when MS-DOS completes the execution of a batch file, you are immediately returned to Windows. If your batch file produces output, you will most likely want to be able to see the information it produces. The simplest technique for displaying the output is to include a PAUSE command in the batch file after the command that produces the information. Another technique is to deselect the Close Window On Exit option in the batch file's PIF so that you must use the EXIT command to return to Windows.

The management of MS-DOS sessions with PIFs is beyond the scope of this book, but this chapter provides a glimpse of how you might use batch files to increase your control over MS-DOS sessions within Windows.

Summary of MS-DOS Exit-Status Values

Several MS-DOS commands provide exit-status values that you can test using IF ERRORLEVEL. The following table lists these values:

Command	Exit-Status Value	Meaning
BACKUP*	0	Successful backup.
	1	No files to back up.
	2	File-sharing conflict; backup incomplete.
	3	User pressed Ctrl-C; backup incomplete.
	4	Fatal error; backup incomplete.
CHKDSK	0	No errors.
	255	Errors detected.
CHOICE**	0	User pressed Ctrl-C .
	255	Error detected.
DEFRAG	0	Successful defragmentation.
	1	Internal error in processing.
	2	No free clusters; DEFRAG needs at least one.
	3	User pressed Ctrl-C; defragmentation incomplete.
	4	General error in processing.
	5	Disk read error.
	6	Disk write error.
	7	Cluster allocation error; use CHKDSK /F.
	8	Memory allocation error.
	9	Insufficient memory.
DELTREE	0	Successful deletion of directory and contents.
DISKCOMP	0	Disks compare exactly.
	1	Disks are not the same.

Command	Exit-Status Value	Meaning
	2	User pressed Ctrl-C; disk compare incomplete.
	3	Unrecoverable read or write error.
	4	Insufficient memory, invalid drive, or syntax error.
DISKCOPY	0	Successful copy.
	1	Nonfatal read or write error.
	2	User pressed Ctrl-C; disk copy incomplete.
	3	Unable to either read source or format target disk.
	4	Insufficient memory, invalid drive, or syntax error.
FIND	0	Successful search (match found).
	1	Search completed (no matches found).
	2	Error during search.
FORMAT	0	Successful format.
	3	User pressed Ctrl-C; format incomplete.
	4	Fatal error; format incomplete.
	5	User pressed N at continue prompt.
GRAFTABL*	0	Table loaded successfully.
	1	Previously loaded table replaced.
	2	No new table loaded.
	3	Invalid command-line parameter.
	4	Incorrect MS-DOS version.
KEYB	0	Successful keyboard load.
	1	Invalid command line.
	2	Invalid keyboard definition table.
	3*	Cannot create table.
	4	CON device error.
	5	Code page not prepared.
	6*	Missing translation table.
	7*	Incorrect MS-DOS version.
MOVE	0	Files moved (or directory renamed) successfully.
	1	Error in moving files or renaming directory.
MSAV	86	Virus detected.

(continued)

(continued)

Command	Exit-Status Value	Meaning
REPLACE	0	Successful replacement.
	2	Source file not found.
	3	Source or target path not found.
	5	Read-only target file.
	8	Insufficient memory.
	11	Invalid command line.
	15*	Invalid disk drive.
RESTORE	0	Successful restore.
	1	No files found.
	3	User pressed Ctrl-C; restore incomplete.
	4	Fatal error; restore incomplete.
SETVER	0	Successful update of version table.
	1	Invalid command-line switch.
	2	Invalid filename.
	3	Insufficient memory.
	4	Invalid version number.
	5	Entry specified not found in table.
	6	MS-DOS system files not found.
	7	Invalid drive.
	8	Too many command-line parameters.
	9	Missing command-line parameter.
	10	Error reading MS-DOS system files.
	11	Version table corrupted in MS-DOS system files.
	12	MS-DOS system files don't support version table.
	13	Insufficient space in version table.
	14	Error writing to MS-DOS system files.
XCOPY	0	Successful copy.
	1	No files found to copy.
	2	User pressed Ctrl-C; copy incomplete.
	4	Initialization error (not enough memory, invalid drive, file or path not found, or syntax error).
	5	Disk write error.

* Not supported in MS-DOS version 6 or later.
**Other values are assigned to characters listed on the command line.

APPENDIX B

Summary of ANSI.SYS Commands

Throughout this reference, we have made extensive use of ANSI.SYS escape sequences. The following table summarizes the ANSI.SYS commands available in MS-DOS versions 6 and later. The left arrow ← represents the escape character, which has an ASCII value of 27.

Sequence	Function
←[*rows*A	Moves cursor up the number of rows specified.
←[*rows*B	Moves cursor down the number of rows specified.
←[*rows*C	Moves cursor right the number of rows specified.
←[*rows*D	Moves cursor left the number of rows specified.
←[*row;col*H	Moves cursor to row and column position.
←[*row;col*f	Same as ←[*row;col*H.
←[s	Saves cursor position.
←[u	Restores cursor position.
←[2J	Clears screen display and places cursor at home position.
←[K	Erases to end of line.
←[*color*m	Sets screen attribute.
←[=*mode*h	Sets video mode.
←[=*mode*l	Resets video mode. (Note that the last character is the lowercase *l*, not the uppercase *I* or the digit *1*.)
←[0;*fkey*; "*string*"p	Defines a function key.

The following table describes the possible values for the *color* parameter in the escape sequence ←[*color*m, which sets the screen attribute:

color Value	Attribute
0	Default color
1	Bold text
2*	Low-intensity text
3*	Italic text
4	Underscore on for IBM monochrome; underscore color (blue) for VGA
5	Blinking text
6*	Rapid-blinking text
7	Reverse-video text
8	Concealed text
30	Black foreground
31	Red foreground
32	Green foreground
33	Yellow foreground
34	Blue foreground
35	Magenta foreground
36	Cyan foreground
37	White foreground
40	Black background
41	Red background
42	Green background
43	Yellow background
44	Blue background
45	Magenta background
46	Cyan background
47	White foreground
48*	Subscript
49*	Superscript

* Not operative on VGA.

NOTE: *Not all values are supported in all versions of ANSI.SYS.*

The following table describes the possible values for the mode parameter in the escape sequence ←[=*mode*h, which sets the video mode:

mode Value	Description
0	40 x 25 monochrome text
1	40 x 25 16-color text
2	80 x 25 monochrome text
3	80 x 25 16-color text
4	320 x 200 4-color graphics
5	320 x 200 monochrome graphics
6	640 x 200 monochrome graphics
7	Enables line wrapping
13	320 x 200 16-color graphics
14	640 x 200 16-color graphics
15	640 x 350 monochrome graphics
16	640 x 350 16-color graphics
17	640 x 480 monochrome graphics
18	640 x 480 16-color graphics
19	320 x 200 256-color graphics

NOTE: ←[=7h *enables line wrapping, and* ←[=7l *disables line wrapping.*

Index

Kris Jamsa

Kris Jamsa is the author of over 40 computer books on a wide range of topics, including MS-DOS, hard-disk management, MS-DOS batch files, Microsoft Windows, graphics, programming languages, WordPerfect, and WordPerfect for Windows. Many of his books have appeared on bestseller lists across the country, and collectively they have sold over one million copies.

Jamsa grew up in Seattle and moved to Phoenix, Arizona, for high school. He received his bachelor's degree in computer science from the United States Air Force Academy in 1983. After graduation, Jamsa worked in Las Vegas as a VAX/VMS system manager for the Air Force. In 1986 he received his master's degree in computer science from the University of Nevada at Las Vegas. Jamsa left the Air Force in 1988 to write full time. He is currently a Ph.D. candidate at Arizona State University, researching multiprocessor operating systems.

He lives in Las Vegas with his wife, Debbie, their daughters, Stephanie and Kellie, and Happy, their dalmatian.